The Heart of Things

'A turn, and we stand in the heart of things'

Robert Browning, 'By the Fire Side'

By A. C. Grayling

The Heart of Things

Applying Philosophy to the 21st Century

A. C. Grayling

Weidenfeld & Nicolson
London

First published in Great Britain in 2005
By Weidenfeld & Nicolson

Extracts from *History of Western Philosophy* © Bertrand Russell 1945
granted with kind permission of Routledge and
The Bertrand Russell Peace Foundation

A CIP catalogue record for this book is
available from the British Library.

ISBN 0 297 84819 4

Typeset, printed and bound in Great Britain by
Butler and Tanner Ltd, Frome and London

Weidenfeld & Nicolson
An imprint of the Orion Publishing Group
Orion House, 5 Upper St Martin's Lane,
London WC2H 9EA

Contents

Acknowledgements

These essays first appeared in *The Times, Literary Review, Guardian, Financial Times, Dubliner, Independent on Sunday, New Statesman, Penguin Online* and, in the case of almost all the essays on individual thinkers, as prefaces to Folio Society editions of their works. I am grateful to all these publications for the opportunity to air these thoughts in their pages and to the editors of *The Times* Weekend Review, the *Dubliner* and the Folio Society for agreement to reprint here. Warm thanks also go to Catherine Clarke, Naomi Goulder and Alan Samson.

Introduction

'And a nod is as good as a wink to the wise,' says an old proverb, and one meaning of this is that to the receptive mind a hint is as good as – and often perhaps better than – a treatise. I say 'often perhaps better' because something that prompts thought without overwhelming it, coercing it, or drowning it in excessive detail, has something to recommend it – not least because it allows the thought in question to develop into something that is the thinker's own.

The miscellany to follow is one of nods and winks in just this spirit. It takes a certain ingenuous faith – but I have it – to believe that people who read and reflect will more likely than not come to judge things with liberality and truth. Part of what such people do is to engage in conversation – with themselves, with other people, with the books they read, with the ideas they contemplate – and it is this conversation that leads to the good. The essays in the following miscellany are conversational contributions likewise – conversational contributions not academic dissertations, consisting for the most part of short pieces that aspire only to suggest or observe.

Almost everyone wishes to live a life that is satisfying and fulfilling, in which there is achievement and pleasure, and which has the respect of people whose respect is worth having. Such a life is one that adds value – to the experience of the person living it, and to the world that the person occupies. To add value to things involves making good choices. To make good choices requires being informed and reflective. To be both these things one must read, enquire, debate and consider.

the best ways of adding value to the world is to be
and fulfilled – let us for short say: happy. Being happy
nse is by itself a good, and it has the marvellously
lition that it is impossible to be truly happy when
people around you are not; for our natural sympathies make the
happiness of others a part of our own. This fact is a logical
function of another fact, which is that we are essentially –
crucially, inescapably – social creatures, which means that the
good life for any individual is one that in significant part has to
be connected to a community effort to create the good society –
the society where individual good lives can flourish.

Do not be misled into thinking that this is saccharine sentiment merely. All you have to do is think of your neigh-
bourhood hit by rockets, raked by machine-gun fire, without
food or clean water, real danger all around, corpses and scream-
ing children everywhere; and contrast this vision with another –
that of a sunny day in a peaceful town where there are theatres
and bookshops, schools and art galleries, all accessible to the
residents, enhancing and enriching their lives. Go on: really feel
the difference.

Really feeling the difference is something that hard experience
makes possible; but it is also made possible by engaging in the
conversation about the good. To repeat: the essays that follow,
loosely grouped by theme into reflections on personal life, on
public life, on some thinkers and on some ideas, are offered as
contributions to that conversation, because they stem from
opportunities to comment and react, review and reflect, which
their author's professional life offers him. It is modestly and
sincerely done, as the short essay form itself attests; because
that form can pretend to nothing definitive, but only to offer
remarks from a point of view.

The thinkers I write about in the third section of this miscellany were all contributors to this conversation about the
good life. They were not merely technical types, introverted
academics careless of the responsibility that their opportunities

to read and think imposed upon them, but people engaged with their fellows and their times – a healthful thing for thought, because it gives thought real content. The essays here began as prefaces to their works, and the hope is that they will serve so still.

This is the fourth in a series of essay miscellanies, all devoted to the conversation about the human condition and the good, whether from a personal or public perspective – these perspectives anyway being intimately linked. None of the volumes requires any of the others as preface, for each is self-standing; but the perennial themes are not remote from any of them, and readers of the others will recognise that there is one main chain of linkage: an attitude, consisting in a belief that everything best about the human heart and mind can help their best prevail, and the hope that it will.

Personal Themes

Happiness

How is happiness attained? Debating this question was, for centuries, the province of philosophers and priests. More recently the topic became, in contrasting style, one of the staples of women's magazines, which did not so much debate as legislate, although the subtext of advertisements they carried said: 'Happiness belongs to those who are thin and buy things'.

Then the pollsters began to investigate what percentage of a given population felt happy, or satisfied, or rated their 'quality of life' highly; and vice versa. The 'World Values Survey', which began in 1995, makes periodic international comparisons of 'satisfaction', the latest showing that the 'most satisfied' people live in Western Europe and both Americas, while the 'least satisfied' live in Eastern Europe.

Lately this kind of information has begun to attract more attention from politicians and policy advisers, and (because it was inevitable that the social sciences should at last bring the question into the laboratory) at the same time 'happiness studies' have become a serious enterprise even at reputable universities. There are now Professors of Happiness Studies, and Quality of Life Institutes, and there is even an academic publication, the *Journal of Happiness Studies*.

The recent flood of statistical information about what does

and does not make people happy ranges from (a) the blindingly obvious: American schoolchildren are less happy at school than when vacationing, less happy alone than with friends; through (b) the interesting-because-confirming: the upward graph of income in Western countries since 1950 is accompanied by a straight line for reported subjective satisfaction, showing that more money does not mean more happiness; to (c) the surprising: the world's happiest people are Nigerians and Mexicans. (But this is not so surprising: both countries are home to highly superstitious cultures revolving upon a popular form of Christianity that has absorbed aboriginal polytheistic and animistic elements. The touch-wood character of the religion is coupled with lack of moral anxiety because salvation is believed to be within easy reach. The combination is an agreeable one for the uncritical.)

Cultural contrasts come to the fore in this plethora of happiness facts. Consider the difference between Japan and the United States. In the former, life satisfaction is gained by meeting family and social expectations, maintaining self-discipline and a friendly and co-operative attitude. In the United States it is gained by self-expression, by feelings of self-worth, and by material success.

If there is anything genuinely surprising about the results of so many questionnaires in so many countries, it is that the old saw about the unhappiness-inducing character of material desires seems to be true after all. People who care particularly about income and status are more dissatisfied, and tend to suffer more from illness, depression and stress, than those who place less weight on these things – so the questionnaires tell us. The source of the problem seems to be the invidiousness of comparisons: if an individual feels that he compares unfavourably (in income, image and standing) with a target group, he will be unhappy.

One route to happiness, therefore, is to stop peering over the fence at the Joneses. That does not mean accepting that one cannot do better or have aspirations; but the comparison should be with oneself only.

The same studies also show that two key factors in life-satisfaction are a sense of being in control of one's own life, and a sense of being valued for what one does. These factors are independent of income and rank. They suggest that a society's aim should be to ensure democracy, employment and job security rather than to goad people into productivity by league tables and performance-based criteria for pay and rank. Creating competitive dissatisfaction as the motivating force in people's lives not only undermines happiness, but is a recipe for social instability, not least because of the inequalities that result. Inequality, social unrest, low subjective satisfaction: leaving aside the question which is the chicken and which the egg, the correlation is persistent and unsurprising.

A problem with methodology in the social sciences is that, however careful and clever a study's research design, what it reveals is correlations rather than causes. Social unrest could cause or be caused by personal dissatisfaction; noting that the two are covariants does not say which is responsible. And in this arena what one wants is causal explanations.

'The happy life', wrote Seneca two millennia ago, 'is a life that is in harmony with its own nature.' He was an exponent of the Stoic philosophy, which taught that the best life is one lived by those who have mastered themselves, have learned wisdom from experience, are steadfast in action, and are always courteous and considerate towards others. To be courageous, energetic, capable of fortitude, and attentive to the good things of the world without being their slave – that, said Seneca, is the recipe for happiness. There is little in the advice he gives about wealth or status, and nothing about performance targets and league tables. The old wisdom and the results of modern questionnaires seem, after all, to have much in common.

Given this, perhaps it would pay to put to one side the questionnaires, advertisers and social scientists, and to reconsider the question of happiness as Seneca prompts us to: from a philosophical point of view.

Everyone wishes to be happy; it is the ultimate goal of all but a few odd folk among whom, bizarrely, might be one or two who actively desire misery. But although all who seek to be happy have ideas about what would make them so, they also suspect that the secret of 'true' happiness is elusive, which is why, in amongst the conventional nostrums for happiness, creeps the cold finger of dissatisfaction and anxiety.

The first lesson of happiness is that the surest way to be unhappy is to think that happiness can be directly sought. The fact is that happiness is an epiphenomenon – that is, something that arises as a by-product of other things, and is only ever a by-product. It comes unconsciously and from the side; it is not and can never be a direct target. It is like the dot of light in a dark room which, if looked at directly, is invisible, but which comes into view when one directs one's gaze elsewhere.

And what it is a by-product of is those activities that are worthwhile in themselves, that bring satisfaction and achievement in the doing, that give one a sense of well-doing and well-being. Enjoyment of leisure, of friendship, of beautiful things and places, of success, are invariable manufacturers of happiness. In the full flush of these things one may not even realise one is happy: the realisation might come retrospectively; but it is a fact about happiness that one can have it without knowing it at the time.

The philosophers of antiquity thought that although it is obvious that (almost) everyone desires happiness, it is far less obvious what happiness actually consists of, and that therefore it is necessary to analyse the concept to see what it implies. Aristotle described it as what attends the life of reason and practical wisdom. Epicurus said that it is the fruit of moderation and quietness. The Stoics said that it is the peace of mind that comes from self-mastery and the philosophical acceptance of life's externally imposed and inescapable vicissitudes, such as illness, grief, failure and death. They all agreed that happiness attends the reflective life of restraint and proportion, based on the right attitude to life: for life's value to us, as Antoine de Saint-Exupéry much later observed, lies not in external things but in how we face them.

Some of the major religions have taken a quite different view of happiness, saying that although there is no certainty that it will be found in this vale of tears, it will assuredly come posthumously to those who keep the straight way. Thus happiness is a state attainable in another dispensation of things, not here (meaning: the human lifetime) where the flesh is vulnerable and evils abound – unless the felicity of the afterlife can be replicated, to some extent anyway, by the steadfast exercise of purity and self-denial. There is a psychological insight at work here: the complete devotee of anything will find much happiness in the state, because self-abnegation is very liberating. But this premises the rejection of much in the human condition, not the embrace of it; which underlies the contrasting view of humanism.

This contrasting view, with its roots in classical antiquity and its fruits in Renaissance and Enlightenment thought, says that autonomy is the basis of the good life. The individual who lives under self-chosen and self-imposed laws that answer to his sense of the obligations of humanity and fellowship, and appreciation of the value of knowledge, art and nature, is in the best position to find happiness, because it is what must attend the endeavour to live wisely through that striving for well-doing and well-being mentioned earlier. The aim of such a life is the achievement of worthwhile goals: happiness rewards the activity of seeking to achieve, whether or not it succeeds.

The Good Life

No man loses any life but this that he now lives.
MARCUS AURELIUS

Prior to Socrates' time, philosophers in ancient Greece devoted their exquisite spirit of enquiry to theorising about the nature and origins of the world. Socrates shifted attention away from those speculations to the question, 'What is the best kind of life?' His question reflected something dramatically new in the history of Western civilisation. To see what it is, recall the last play in Aeschylus's Oresteian trilogy. In it Orestes is pursued by the Furies because he has killed his mother in revenge for her killing his father Agamemnon. He appeals to the goddess Athene for help, whereupon she summons a jury of Athenian citizens to try his case. He is acquitted, to the fury of the Furies, who say to Athene, 'You young gods have usurped our privileges; we pursue revenge, but here you have assembled a jury which has acquitted him.' Athene replies, 'We are in a new world; we can no longer appeal to the warrior virtues, relying on might for right and revenge for justice. In our new world people must be civilised, and resolve problems by co-operation and agreement.' Thus Aeschylus captures a crucial moment of change, a shift of reliance from warrior virtues to civic virtues. Socrates' question: 'How should we live?' is central to that shift.

What Socrates discovered, and what philosophers, writers and artists increasingly realised as a result of the tradition of thought he started, is well captured by the Enlightenment, defined by Immanuel Kant as the state in which people take responsibility for themselves, and exercise autonomy, the opposite of which, namely heteronymy, characterises life lived under the government of something external – gods, ancient scriptures, absolute monarchs, traditions, the blood of the nation – in short, an external source of authority that obliges the individual to live as it requires.

The Enlightenment ideal, although making autonomy central, also celebrates the essentially social character of human beings: people live in communities, and their relationships are among the most important things they have. Kant's insight comes down to saying that the good life is the chosen life, lived in rich and satisfying relation to others. When Socrates said, 'The life truly worth living is the considered life,' he meant a life which is well informed, has worthwhile goals, and is lived discerningly so that one can respond to others well, and live flourishingly for oneself.

The foregoing remarks straddle the centuries between Socrates and Kant because something quite different lay between the debate about ethics in classical antiquity and the revival of that debate in the modern period, which started in the seventeenth century. This of course is the fact that from the fourth century AD until the Reformation a hegemony over thought was exercised by the Christian religion. The Church had a definite idea about how people should live, what the aim of life is, and how happiness is to be obtained. Part of this view was that happiness, at any rate in the full sense, is secured by living so that one survives into a posthumous existence in which one will be permanently in the presence of God's glory, and therefore will enjoy bliss for ever. In the mortal dispensation of the flesh, one might suffer and undergo the agonies of the 'vale of tears'. There was an extensive *contemptus mundi* (contempt of the world) literature in medieval times, so called because it premised the idea of the world as a place of disease, suffering and disappointment, where life is short, nasty and brutish; so courage in keeping the faith is what ultimately opens the gates into true happiness lying beyond the boundaries of death.

But both classical and modern thought take a different focus: not upon the transcendent, but upon this present life, premising the idea that it is possible to have happiness and fulfilment now, in this world; that life is not something which is about to happen, next week or somewhere else, but which is happening now; and therefore this is the moment to grasp, and this is the place to be happy.

When the debate about these matters revived at the beginning of the modern period, it narrowed its focus for a time from what the ancients properly described as 'ethics' to what we now call 'morality'. Morality is of course part of ethics, but it is not the whole of ethics. Morality is about some of our responsibilities to others, whereas ethics is about one's 'ethos', one's whole way of life. It is about what sort of person one is. The point can be clearly put by noting that it is an ethical matter what colour you paint your house, but it is not a moral matter. What colour you paint your house says something about you, your choices, and how you express of yourself – in short, your way of being you. Morality is part of that, but without the rest it is only half as good.

As a result of the Enlightenment, ideas of individual rights, of transparent and accountable institutions of government, and of opportunities for people to exercise a fulfilling autonomy, steadily became more general. As that has happened so the idea of ethics in the broader ancient sense has revived, and in the contemporary world people now think – even if they do so only implicitly – that how they live is an all-embracing concern, determining what they are and the overall quality of their lives.

People who live in relatively peaceful and stable parts of the world, who eat regularly and keep warm in winter, and who have many opportunities to exercise their human needs for creativity, enjoyment, friendship and the acquisition of knowledge, are very privileged historically speaking. It means that they have the chance, if only they will take it, to be genuinely happy – providing they also work to try to make happier those who are less fortunate than themselves: for happiness cannot be complete if it co-exists with indifference to those who do not share it.

Wealth

A ristotle described wealth as 'whatever money can buy'. This is a surprising definition in two ways. First, it is standard now to define wealth in terms of money itself rather than what it can be exchanged for. It is expressed as how much a person or country is worth – hence the term 'millionaire'. Yet it is obvious that a man who has a million pounds untouched in a bank, and lives in a miserly hovel on bread and beans for fear of reducing his hoard, is the poorest wretch alive. In contrast, a person with a tenth of that sum who uses it to buy books and art, to go to the theatre, to travel, and to entertain his friends, is thereby vastly the richer. This, so far, proves Aristotle right.

But secondly, Aristotle's definition surprisingly leaves out the fact, known to all, that there are many kinds of wealth money cannot buy. You can buy education, but you cannot buy intelligence; you can buy designer clothes, but not style; cosmetics, but not beauty; sex, but not love. Doubtlessly, money can buy help towards style, beauty and love. But since it is the amenities themselves that are the true wealth, a fact that the great philosopher elsewhere acknowledges, it is an oddity that he did not include them in his definition.

'There is a time when a man distinguishes the idea of felicity from the idea of wealth; it is the beginning of wisdom,' said Emerson. Here Emerson is using 'wealth' in the conventional sense of money in quantity, although he would doubtless agree with the coiners of proverbs – who remind us that health is the true wealth, and that riches do not satisfy but instead increase our appetites – that we do better to reserve the word for what is really worth having, and consign mere bulk of cash, unless it is well and liberally spent, to the category of disease.

In this respect Sa'di is right to say that 'riches are intended for the comfort of life, not life for the hoarding of riches'. To spend is to gain; but of course, only if what is bought is not the equipment or occasion for empty ostentation. It is obvious from ten miles away when quantity of cash outstrips quantity of sense – a stretch limo is a symptom of that state, along with the junk and glitter of the lifestyle it transports – and in such cases what money has bought is lost opportunity.

In most times and places a large bank balance is taken to be the chief mark of achievement. But if what is counted is not the figures on a bank statement but things learned, done, seen and enjoyed in the course of a life – in short, if we counted what was spent, not what remains – we would have a truer evaluation of the wealth in a person's possession.

No doubt all this sounds frightfully earnest, and so it is; but no apology is needed, for the question of how to live genuinely well is a significant one, given that we each have one life only, and that lives last on average less than a thousand months. It therefore matters to know how to live richly, which in turn means knowing what true wealth is. Prevailing views about the desirability of getting and having lots of money are the result of the usual attention-span deficit which truncates 'having money is good because of what you can do and be as a result' into 'having money is good', so that when any surplus eventuates, the only things its possessors can think to spend it on are banal gestures, sequins and gilt, size and noise, excess, inebriation and parade.

It is enchanting to dream of what one would do with a sizeable lottery win – more than the kind that would merely pay off the mortgage and the washing machine. If you would know yourself or others, enquire what that dream would be. Almost nothing is as revealing as what, in the absence of the means, a person chooses as ends.

Quality of Life

If such a thing as paradise existed, it would be defined by having none of the disadvantages of its advantages. It would provide abundance without making anyone satiated or fat; and it would provide pleasure without making anyone bored or diseased. It would be a perfect place equipped in perfect ways to offer happiness, fulfilment and well-being to all who cared to benefit, without cost. It would do that seemingly impossible-because-contradictory thing of meeting everyone's wishes – and that includes competing wishes – simultaneously.

It is a commonplace now, but a true one and infinitely worth iterating, that prosperity brings problems, notable among them pollution, congestion and obesity. Central to debate about this worthy commonplace is an abstract concept, but an important one: the idea of 'quality of life'. In paradise, life is all quality; in the real world, as yet more fruits of wealth fall into our grasp, the problems they bring with them worsen. It is a Faustian contract, in which sunlight does not shine without multiplying shadows elsewhere.

The phrase 'quality of life' once exclusively denoted environmental concerns. Clean air and water, noise abatement, control of rubbish and vermin, provision of parks and playgrounds – such were the first desiderata, and nothing has diminished their importance. They once – in other centuries – used not to matter. Just think of drains: chamber pots used to be emptied from windows into the street below, and passers-by had to look out for themselves. London acquired a sewage system only when, one hot nineteenth-century summer, the

Thames's filth backed all the way up to Westminster, and its stench penetrated Parliament. An act was rapidly passed, at last reducing East End deaths from typhoid and dysentery.

Environmental improvements continued fitfully thereafter: smokeless fuel ended London's notorious and fatal fogs, unleaded petrol removed one threat to child mental development. But optimism is misplaced. Recent research has revealed a terrible fact: that an average British body carries a cocktail of more than thirty toxic chemicals, acquired from sofas, carpets, hair sprays, shampoos, computers, non-stick pans, canned foods, TV sets and much besides. The Faustian contract not only persists, but the devil's side is winning: nearly 90 per cent of the 100,000 chemicals in industrial use in Europe have been insufficiently researched for their human toxicity, and their use is growing in the relentless pursuit of providing 'competitive' (read 'cheap') transport, food, clothing, and much else.

Government action is obviously appropriate in these matters. Is it also appropriate for obesity and smoking? Some say these involve personal choice and responsibility only, and that thinking otherwise has civil-liberty implications. But both take billions from the taxpayer and the economy every year in health costs; so here public and private concerns compete. Bernard Mandeville, whose 'Fable of the Bees' anticipated Adam Smith's theories, said that private vices (greed and other appetites) produce public benefits (wealth). In this case private vices produce public burdens, giving the public an interest in intervening to promote the corresponding virtue.

Mention of private choices reminds one that there is a whole other dimension to debates about quality of life. As the philosophical tradition has consistently taught, the true quality of anyone's life is primarily a question of how it is lived, what goals it serves, and what principles govern it, irrespective of external factors. Rome's poet of the good life, Horace, gave masterly expression to an ideal he had learned while studying philosophy at Athens: that of the simple life, graced by amity and friendship. 'My prayer is for a garden with flowing water and trees nearby,' he wrote. In the conditions of his time – Rome in the last century BC – the idea of a retreat far from the dangerous world of the capital was not only an attractive but a feasible one.

In the tumult of contemporary Western life an Horatian idyll might still be possible, but only for a few – mainly and paradoxically, those rich enough to afford it, or those who can find wealth of experience in poverty. Unless, of course, the idyll is understood symbolically – and in fact Horace intended this, for he described his philosophic retreat as even more a state of mind than a physical place. And given the pollutions of thought and emotion generated by the contemporary world's heat, noise and affray, such a thing is obviously more than just a possibility: it is a possession to covet.

Manners

In a world of atrocities and conflicts, suicide bombings, assassinations, wars, torture, genocide and ethnic cleansing, where can one find a basis for morality? The answer is surprisingly simple though easily forgotten. It lies in the minor transactions of ordinary life; for, given that morality fundamentally concerns how we treat each other, its starting point is: good manners.

Manners have a bad press among cynics, who variously describe them as the most acceptable form of hypocrisy or, at best, a fictitious form of benevolence. They have even been dismissed on the grounds that only unattractive people need them (this, predictably, was said by Evelyn Waugh, who added in explanation, 'the pretty can get away with anything').

Such views are profoundly mistaken. Manners are central to the true morality; they are the lubricant of social relations, the sweetener of personal intercourse, and the softener of conflict. Without them society itself would be impossible. Answers to questions about how a complex, pluralistic community should cope with the stresses of internal difference and competition have to put civility at their heart, because nothing else – certainly not the blunt instrument of law nor the despairing council of social apartheids – can do nearly as well.

It is a mistake to confuse manners with etiquette. Knowing the rituals of decorum and precedence, and what cutlery to use in what order at dinner, or how genteelly to peel one's apple with a knife and fork, are all very well in their way; but such niceties too readily collapse into affectation, like raising the little finger when drinking, and worrying about whether to pour milk into the cup before or after the tea. Such things are irrelevant beside the real point of manners, which is – quite simply – to treat others with consideration. And that might often involve forgetting etiquette, especially when the latter is used as a device to snub and exclude. It was once well said that rudeness is the weak man's imitation of strength, but when the mere appearance of manners is used as a form of rudeness too, they become their own negation.

Etiquette had its origins in bringing pleasantness to the necessities of communal living. Reformers of behaviour at table, for example, managed to bring about the relative peace and democracy of today's dinner hour from what was once a ravening, every-man-for-himself event where meat was torn from carcasses by hand, bones were tossed to the floor, spitting and various unmentionable activities took place right there at the board as eating and drinking proceeded – a species of gustatory mayhem, premised on imperatives of quantity and haste. And what was characteristic of the table was even more so of the street, once as much a public lavatory as a path between destinations.

Castiglione was one of the tamers of such grossness, advising his contemporaries how to comport themselves better, for example by not scratching their lice in public. But he recognised that, although etiquette is an expression of manners, it is not only not the whole of manners, but neither necessary to them nor a substitute for them. For he too saw that the point of manners is, fundamentally, consideration, and his pleasing descriptions of the ideal Renaissance individual – a rounded personality possessing taste and a well-informed mind, habituated to graceful treatment of others based on thoughtfulness about their needs and interests – offer a paradigm of what the well-mannered person should be.

In teaching these lessons Castiglione was not being original; he was in fact reprising the concept of the 'great-souled individual' central to Aristotle's idea of ethics. Aristotle taught that the good person is one who takes each demand for moral decision on its own merits, and tries to find the best path through the case, applying practical wisdom and experience, and seeking to avoid the vices that stand on either side of the right course of action – as cowardice and rashness hem courage from opposite quarters, and as meanness and profligacy flank generosity. A person who tries to do the courageous, the generous, the wise thing whenever he can is 'great-souled'. The Greek for this is the alarming-sounding *megalopsychos*, it is from its Latin equivalent *magna anima* that our word 'magnanimous' comes.

English translations of Aristotle rendered *megalopsychos* as 'gentleman' – not to denote a person holding a social rank by accident of birth, but the sort of person colloquially described as 'a real gent'. It is thus the real gent – the civil individual – whose behaviour binds society together. Happily, such people abound, and good-mannerly acts therefore happen millions of times every day, which is why society generally works. It is only the ill-mannered few – the uncivil minority: among them criminals and thugs, murderers and fanatics – who make things seem otherwise.

Reading

Reading is one of the essentials – essentials, note: not merely one of the appurtenances or amenities – of the good life. For it is not just the familiar pleasures that come from responsive reading that matter, but the effects of these on how we live our lives, and what kinds of communities we accordingly create. This point is not always fully appreciated, so one must take Wittgenstein's advice to 'assemble reminders' and tell everyone who will listen that reading is more than they think it is.

The point at issue can be made in connection with other narrative forms too. But novels are the paradigm because reading is an especially focused experience, unfolding in private time, and one that makes a fundamental difference. A play cannot be stopped and reprised in the way that pages can be re-read, whether to relish something good or understand something better. A novel is all present at once, and can be gone over and back, re-entered, skimmed, sampled or devoured, just as required. This adds to the value of its contents. But it is the contents, of course, that matter most.

Obviously enough, many novels do not aspire to do more than amuse, please, offer escape and refreshment. But even with this modest ambition they provide several significant opportunities to anyone who will read attentively. One is the opportunity to consider one's own experience, seeing in the mirror of the story reflections of one's world, and the universal aspects of oneself, at the revealing angles that result from seeing them refracted into other guises.

Another is the opportunity to peer into experiences one has

not had, and might well never have, in other lives and ways of life. This opportunity is immeasurable. Being restricted to personal experience and the observation only of people in one's immediate circle is no bar to becoming perceptive and wise. But being a fly on the wall in a far wider array of times and places, observing very different lives and thereby having the chance to spectate, and perhaps even sympathise with, choices and desires that have never occurred to one, or are not part of one's own repertoire – that is the gift that comes from thoughtful reading even of averagely good novels. The better the novel, the richer the possibilities it offers in this as in all its other dimensions (of pleasure-giving and the like). Perhaps 'great literature' is literature which, among its other qualities, best discloses to us different worlds, or deeper aspects of our own world, and teaches us how to feel more generously, discriminate more finely, and understand more comprehensively as a result.

These things matter for a special reason: they promise an enlargement of our sympathies. That, to repeat, is by far not the only thing novels do for us, and it is not the only way our sympathies can be educated and expanded; but it is an exceedingly powerful way, and throughout human history storytelling has been a central means of informing people about possibilities beyond their personal sphere, and inviting them to understand those possibilities better.

And the enlargement of our sympathies matters crucially, because sympathy is the basis of moral community. To sympathise with others is to understand their interests, needs and choices, and to see these as relevant to decisions about one's own choices. It is also, and more, to see others as having a claim on one's concern, just as one expects to be taken into account by others in turn. When these mutualities are in place, society functions far better than just adequately. Because reading promotes insight into oneself and others, it thereby helps promote the good life in the good society.

Attitudes

No one can avoid being a target of terrorism, not even those who cannot possibly have had a quarrel with anyone, such as the many children who have been among terrorism's victims in attacks all over the world.

Given this, how should individual non-combatant citizens fight terrorism – apart, obviously, from being vigilant about suspicious packages in public places? The answer is: by their attitude. Attitude is very consequential stuff. It determines everything one does, from falling in love to voting for one candidate rather than another. As Antoine de Saint-Exupéry said, 'The meaning of things lies not in things themselves, but in our attitudes towards them.'

A natural attitude to take towards those who commit indiscriminate mass murder in the name of their chosen ideology or faith is contempt. Some observe that it takes intelligence to plan, and courage to carry out, a terrorist atrocity; but that dignifies matters too far (there hardly seems anything brave about killing defenceless civilians of all ages). The very idea of blowing up a crowd of unsuspecting strangers because you hate them in the abstract, or their government, or the culture to which they belong, smacks of something subhuman, something morally cretinous: a kind of moral subnormality so lacking in imagination or human sympathy that it can set at nothing the theft of a random number of lifetimes, while condemning many more lifetimes – those left behind – to grief.

It is of course a matter of attitude for the morally cretinous too. But what an attitude! Imagine some people eating breakfast, taking their children to school, choosing books at the library, concentrating on computer screens at work, planning to visit their parents next weekend; then imagine (try to imagine) suddenly and gratuitously killing them for no better reason than that they hold a certain nationality, live in a certain part of the world, or do not share one's religion. Is this imaginable? Not for a normal person. Only by means of a twisted attitude, something that has ceased to be the human attitude and become a function of perversion, hatred and cruelty, can it become so. What are the historical precedents? They include Hitler's henchmen and Stalin's executioners. Well: one sees that terrorist organisers of suicide bombings in cafés and trains are in good company.

At the same time it would be a mistake to underestimate the practicality of such people. The nature of some of the major atrocities that ushered in the twenty-first century bespeaks a thought-provoking degree of organisation, money, infrastructure and personnel. No doubt, in the shadowy world of terrorism and counter-terrorism, the activities of security forces have often wittingly or otherwise foiled terrorist endeavours. But the inescapable fact is that while terrorists exist and can acquire the means, their atrocities will occur; and each of our safeties rests in the lap of statistics alone.

Contempt for the moral cretins is therefore only the start. The more significant attitude to have is: to go on living as if (apart from a few obvious and rational precautions) the moral cretins do not exist. If we change our lives, our laws, our open societies, our habits of civilised freedom and mutual trust, because there are a few terrorists in the world who will anyway assuredly manage to kill a tiny percentage of us from time to time, no matter what we do, then we will have surrendered the victory to them. What they want is for us to share their bleak and impoverished world-view. We should refuse, no matter what they do.

Even if (as doubtless they will) they get nuclear bombs and set them off in the middle of some of our big cities, they will only be able to kill a minority of us, even if that minority numbers hundreds of thousands. We are sixty million in Britain, over half a billion in 'the West', six billion in the world as a whole: there is futility in the project of hatred that the bombers have launched. So the right attitude to take towards them is to recognise that their worst can never be more than a snowball thrown at a castle – the castle of our values and our freedoms.

Pride

Followers of sport know that it is full of prompts to philosophical reflection, despite appearances. These latter seem to be all about sweat and effort, even broken bones at times; but the reality behind them has much to do with three human characteristics which can be great virtues: courage, commitment and pride. Even when defeated, an individual or team that manifests the first two thereby earns a right to the third, which is a kind of victory after all.

Here, though, is a paradox. The sporting person's pride is a good thing, well earned; yet pride is one of the seven deadly sins. The crime for which Lucifer was cast from heaven was pride, and the proud are warned that they will come to a bad end: 'Pride goeth before destruction,' says Proverbs, 'and an haughty spirit before a fall.' Clearly there are two concepts in play here, bearing the same name. When that is the case the first rule of philosophy comes into play: draw a distinction.

And who better to help one do it than Jane Austen. Among her many excellences, Austen is a subtle student of moral epistemology. In *Pride and Prejudice* she explores the mutual misperceptions of Elizabeth Bennet and Mr Darcy, the former in thinking the latter intolerably proud, the latter prejudicially thinking the former too low-born.

Darcy recognises his mistake more quickly than Elizabeth recognises hers. He is forced to grasp the truth of what he knew only as a platitude, namely, that virtues of character are more important than social station. So even though the insufferable Mrs Bennet comes with the package, he cannot help loving

Elizabeth. For her part, she has to see Pemberley, Fitzwilliam Darcy's splendid country seat, to understand that what she took to be Luciferian pride is in fact the duty owed to an important responsibility (as conceived in early nineteenth-century terms), namely, to preserve and then pass on a name and a great inheritance.

Elizabeth had failed to see that the pride which belongs to that family of concepts which includes arrogance, vanity and smugness is not the same as the pride which belongs to that family of concepts which includes self-worth, success and confidence. The difference lies between the pride which says, 'I would rather eat grass standing up than roast beef kneeling down,' and the pride which makes a generation stiff-necked.

Pride is an emotion of self-assessment, along with shame and guilt. Such emotions as anger, hatred and grief are typically directed at external objects, mainly other people, though psychotherapy has long since taught people to recognise that they can be the targets of their own anger and hatred too. (We take that to be obvious now; it has only been so since Freud.) Emotions of self-assessment involve beliefs about what other people think about us, or might think if they knew our secrets. And this in turn involves a scale of 'better' and 'worse' against which we measure ourselves, so that we can be proud or ashamed even when others know nothing of what prompts either feeling.

This inner scale underlies our feelings of confidence or insecurity. At a guess, most people live with the mistaken belief that other people's lives are going much better than their own lives are, and for that reason they feel vaguely ashamed about not having achieved as much, earned as much, or otherwise 'as muched' as their friends, neighbours or siblings. The translation into popular psychology of the insight that it is, for these reasons, a common human foible to lack confidence, has produced the irritating American habit of making everyone believe, irrespective of justification, that they are 'worth it' ('because', so the hair-shampoo advertisements say, 'I'm worth it'.) This represents a confusion between the two senses of pride at stake. A key to what we might for a moment call Darcian pride is that it is supposed to be rooted in a form of merit – not one we would now much recognise, for in Austen's world it is a merit of birth – while Luciferian pride is rooted in arrogance and false superiority.

Self-Interest

Albert Camus said that the fundamental philosophical question is: 'Should I commit suicide?' If the answer is 'No' it is because there is a reason to live: there is something worth having, doing or being, which gives purpose to life, and thereby makes it valuable.

But there is another fundamental philosophical question too. It is: 'How far am I my brother's keeper?' This question lies implicitly in the background when anyone's choices or actions affect others. The question can be variously rephrased. How much must I consider others' interests? What is the degree of my responsibility towards others? These very formulations assume that a certain degree of such responsibility exists – not just to close associates, but to strangers and foreigners too. Only a knave could publicly say otherwise. But the key terms are: how much? to what degree?

Practical examples help to bring the import of such questions home. Consider the following one. When these words were first written, the Arabs of Sudan were perpetrating a horrendous atrocity against the African tribes of Dafur in the west of their country, driving a million of them from their homes, committing mass murder and rape – all in the comfortable assurance that no one in the outside world would lift a finger to stop them.

There is no secret about what happened in the Sudan, though Western news media hardly mentioned it, giving far more attention to football and other equally important matters. Sudan's Arab militia, the Janjaweed, had the express backing of their government, whose helicopters located the fleeing Zaghawa,

Masalit and Fur tribespeople, then directed the militiamen to them. Tribesmen and boys were massacred out of hand, tribeswomen and girls raped and then killed. The refugees – starving, hunted, terrified – hid in the mountains or struggled to reach the safety of Chad, driven by the Janjaweed's relentless savagery.

How much – to what degree – did people elsewhere in the world feel a responsibility to help the victims of this mayhem? On the evidence available as it actually happened, it appeared that very few even asked themselves the question. Oxfam shops had posters in their windows requesting help for the refugees flooding into neighbouring Chad. But where were the French army, the Canadian air force, the people elsewhere in the Arab world so shamed by what their own kind were doing that they hastened to stop it? The absence and the silence were as shocking as the atrocities themselves, for they answered the question about the degree of our responsibility to others by saying: 'None.'

What weighs against our concern for others is self-interest. Appropriate self-interest is a good thing; we have duties to ourselves and those closely associated with us, and taking responsibility for our own well-being is not only to our advantage but, cumulatively, to the good of all – for then we are not a burden on others. But when legitimate and appropriate self-interest turns into indifference or callousness, making us shut our eyes to the claim that others' suffering makes on us, then the world's moral machinery is out of kilter, and in the end threatens our own well-being too. As this suggests, really thoughtful self-interest would give a high priority to concern for others; for selfishness is self-defeating.

To see why, consider the classic example discussed in Game Theory, that of 'the prisoner's dilemma'. Two men are arrested for a serious crime, and are interrogated separately. Each knows that if neither confesses, they will both get a light sentence for associated minor offences. Each knows that if one confesses and the other does not, the confessor will be released but the other will get a life sentence. And each knows that if both confess, both will get twenty years in prison.

Obviously, the best outcome for each individually is secured by confessing, providing that the other does not confess; one gains maximally provided the other loses maximally. But the concomitant risk each individually runs is that both lose maximally. The overall best outcome for both, accordingly, is for neither to confess, so that both get light sentences. Co-operation is therefore the unsurprising route to the optimal result. In the real world the first, selfish, option is chosen far more often than the second co-operative one, most people (and states) gambling on getting the maximum for themselves at others' expense. Since that is also the maximally risky option, is it any surprise that the world is a mess?

This shows what the answer should be to our question, 'How much am I my brother's keeper?' The answer is, 'Almost as much as I am my own keeper.' May that thought always determine what is done about such tragedies as have occurred in the Sudan, the Balkans, Rwanda ... back through a litany of human disgrace to the greatest of them all, the Holocaust, and beyond even to the beginnings of history.

Ancestors

I can trace my ancestry back to a protoplasmal primordial atomic globule.

W. S. GILBERT

When the Public Records Office's 1901 census went online it had been engineered to receive 1.2 million hits a day. The website received 1.2 million hits an hour. The system naturally collapsed, and the multitudes eager to glimpse their forebears in the year of Queen Victoria's death were disappointed.

Whatever the motives people have for researching their family histories, they are assuredly fewer in number than the multitudes of avid amateur historians themselves. It is reflexly assumed that people hope to find themselves related to aristocracy or fame; that is a common motive. More optimistically still, some hope to trace a link to a deceased plutocrat whose estate, swollen in value over the years, lies waiting in Chancery to be claimed. The hope of gain is thus another, though doubtless infrequent, motive. But surely the chief motive is frank and worthy curiosity about the people who are in effect part of oneself – who they were, what they were like, what they did, and why. History cannot be an abstraction when it becomes personal. To see a picture of one's great-grandmother as a girl, to handle a grandfather's medals, to visit places built, farmed or owned by forebears, is to make the past palpable and vivid.

The good news for the curious is that almost everyone in these islands whose great-grandparents were born here, is almost certainly related to almost everyone else in these islands.

Accordingly we all have aristocratic relations, and can all claim to be connected to William the Conqueror. More to the point, all humanity can claim relationship with a single female – an ur-great-grandmother – who lived a very long time ago at a crucial branching point in the evolutionary history of the human species. And long before her, all living things possessed a single common ancestor, who (or which) was thus the ultimate founder of our line, namely a protoplasmal primordial blob. So all animals are of one ancient family, and all humans – more intimately still – are cousins.

These considerations are not however the point for amateur genealogists. They would like to know about a particular set of people whose connection to them is not merely genetic but such that, at a certain point, it blends with documents and memories, and begins to provide explanations for family circumstances. The curiosity is a good one, because it is a practical application of the spirit of historical enquiry – and seeing into the past is a necessity for seeing the present and future more clearly.

An unworthy interest in ancestry revolves upon taking pride in being descended from some great figure, as if his or her achievements magically shed lustre on oneself. Curiously, most of the most ancient aristocratic families owe their first rise into prominence to rapine and robbery, and yet their descendants preen themselves on belonging to 'older' families than those whose founders were ennobled for service to the state, or to science or the arts. Either way, what ancestors did is no reason for descendants to puff themselves up, unless they independently merit doing so through their own achievements.

In other traditions interest in ancestors is not a question of snobbery but is based on the belief that they influence the present, benevolently or malignly, and therefore need to be remembered, tended, even fed and supplied with ghost money for their needs in the other world. Ancestor worship, or at least respect, is widespread in history and among cultures. Central

America has its exotic Day of the Dead, which chiefly involves the enjoyment of a lavish and happy flower-bedecked picnic among the family graves in the cemetery. China has its Qing Ming (Clear and Bright) festival at the beginning of spring, when the ancestral graves are swept and foodstuffs left upon them – roast pig is a favourite with ghosts – and garlands are laid and kites flown. Japan has its Obon, or Festival of the Dead, when for several evenings people suspend lit paper lanterns in their local cemetery, painted with the family insignia to guide their forebears' spirits back to the incense-wreathed *ohaka* (the family tomb). Ancient Roman households each had their shrine to ancestor spirits – although by historical times these had become little more than good-luck amulets, like horseshoes today (or in Roman times themselves, carvings of erect penises over the front door).

If family history and respect for ancestors has a practical value, it lies in making us think about how we ourselves can be good ancestors – in respect of protecting the environment for future people, and not leaving scars that might prompt future conflicts or wars between them.

Self-Restraint

Each year hundreds of thousands of Americans have an operation to staple their stomachs and shorten their small intestines in order to lose weight. The operations are effective; those who undergo them lose an average of 100 pounds (7 stones). They are too effective for some; post-operative readmissions to hospital for malnutrition and liver failure began to rise fast soon after the operation became commonplace.

It is said that if one wishes to look into the future, one should look at contemporary America. That was no longer true for everything by the beginning of the twenty-first century, notably in science and technology, in which the Far East and Europe had by then again outstripped the United States on most indicators (there were for example, more papers by Chinese authors in international physics journals than by American ones). But it is certainly true for obesity, which increases rapidly wherever prosperity rises; and fastest of all in Britain, where the rise in obesity rates is second only to that of America.

A well-known observation is that the trend is not unconnected with proliferation of American-style fast-food outlets and beverages. Abundant, ubiquitous, very cheap food packed with ingredients that animal taste buds are geared to crave, namely fat, salt and sugar, has created an epidemic of disease in the rich world, at the same time laying waste to nature as immense tonnages of beef on the hoof are ranched where forests once stood. Every year 10,000 square miles of Amazon rainforest are cleared (nearly ten Cornwalls in area) to accommodate the growing numbers of cattle required.

The connection of events thus portrayed, between Amazonian trees crashing to the ground and people hospitalised for inanition because they underwent surgery for obesity, is a spectacular indictment of modern arrangements. If coffins for the victims of obesity were made from the forest's felled trees, a sort of mad poetry would enter the equation. But in the meantime billions of dollars are spent each year on diets, slimming magazines, gym memberships, fads, ersatz foods (imitation bacon, chocolate substitute, sweeteners, 'lo-cal' drinks so huge that they are more calorific than an ordinary glass of juice) – the list is endless.

All this is very well known; and yet it seems not to make a blind bit of difference, for the network of problems is, like incontinent eaters themselves, obviously getting larger, and spreading.

It would seem facile to invoke the ancient Stoic teachings about self-mastery at this juncture, for restraint is truly difficult to practise in connection with something that begins insensibly and grows harder to reverse with time. For the weight-gainer is unwittingly following another famous Stoic precept: 'Follow nature.' In the presence of tasty abundance, the natural response is to gorge, lest famine follow; except that famine never follows in the world's rich countries. Consider the lion: he eats himself into a bloated stupor when opportunity offers, then rests for many days afterwards, taking no more exercise than to flick his tail against flies. (By the way: the first thing he eats, some observers report, is the contents of his kill's stomach – which is to say, vegetable soup, suggesting that he is a vegetarian manqué, condemned to endless steak tartar.)

Getting calories once cost all the calories got. Now, short of gastric bypass or 'duodenal switch', the only sure method of countering the calorie glut is: will power – real will power, teeth-gritting will power – and with it, for a time anyway, misery. When the Stoics preached self-mastery they meant precisely the courage to endure the latter and to sustain the former; and only their way works.

The Marquise du Deffand said of the miracle of St Denis (who, after being decapitated, walked 100 kilometres carrying his head under his arm) that the only difficult thing about his feat was the first step. Alas, that is not true of losing weight. But after a thousand steps it *becomes* true; that is the good news. Every step needs will – there is no getting round the fact; and using will power is exactly what most of us least like doing. But happily, will is a muscle that strengthens with exercise. All the better if that leads to physical exercise, which is literally addictive, prompting secretion of endogenous morphines that induce feelings of pleasure; so that once an exercise routine is established, it is harder to stop than it was to begin.

And the advantage of Stoicism over stomach staples is that it has many other highly profitable uses besides.

Solitude

Solitude is sometimes best society.

MILTON

As essentially communal animals we need to socialise, if only to remind ourselves of our weaknesses. If we always lived alone we would never find ourselves failing, and would never have to face the test of other peoples' needs and demands. Lacking conversation, disagreement, alternative opinions, criticism and challenge, we would become intellectually feeble and morally unready. Moreover, society is the necessary field for the exercise of our human obligations: we cannot honour parents, love children, foster friendships and nurture what gifts we might possess for the benefit of mankind unless we stand, after all, in relation to parents, children, friends, and mankind.

But too much society threatens to be equally debilitating. It makes us dilute our principles in the interests of consensus, it often seduces us into speaking and even thinking in commonplaces, it can lead us to compromise our honour and our ideals. It far too often intimidates to silence the inner voice that whispers our grandest ambitions, and it invariably saps the energy from our emotions until only a handful of them are left in operation with which to manage the whole range of our interactions and responses.

Solitude is the antidote to the world being too much with us in these harmful ways. It consists in the welcome physical absence of others (loneliness, quite differently, is the unwelcome psychological absence of others). It allows us to achieve companionship with ourselves. It is a place of freedom, an expanse of opportunities. It enables us to become discerning again, and reflective. In the crowd of other peoples' thoughts and opinions one's own either get knocked about or they survive by simplifying themselves and waxing assertive. In solitude their shades of grey can resume their luminous, lambent, pearly quality, and grow richer in meaning thereby.

Victorian moralists dispraised solitude in favour of sociability. They thought it an obligation on us to entertain others, to brighten a face or help a companion's hours to pass more pleasantly. The virtues that produce these results are positive ones, whereas the solitary who congratulates himself on having neither said nor done an injurious thing during the course of his day can claim only negative virtue to his merit. 'I did no harm; I told no lie; I did no one an injustice'; what price such laudations, said the Victorian moralist, when the virtue in question comes so cheaply and is so dangerously agreeable to the conscience?

But then, Victorian moralists (a breed that still partially exists among us) required something uphill about morality to make it genuine. It had to be work. There is no virtue in pleasure, for them, and no reward for unearned innocence. Yet the essence of solitude is its vast opportunity for innocence, away from temptations to selfishness and unfairness, while yet offering us rich profit from the chance to catch up with life, and to discover the things we keep secret even from ourselves. That way treasure lies; and solitude is the chest that stores it.

Romance

St Valentine's Day observances are not about love or sex; they are about romance. Romance might be hoped to lead to love, or at least to sex; but the route must not be confused with the destination. Romance is not love, but the dream of love. It is not sex, but the foreplay of foreplay. It occupies the spring of love's year, the rosy dawn of passion's bright day. Its traditional tokens of flowers and chocolates are precisely apt: a flower seduces the bee to its service of fertilisation, and chocolate contains phenethylamine, a chemical produced internally by people undergoing sexual infatuation. Presented together, they might equally aptly evoke a blush in the cheek of the one romanced; for, according to Freud, a blush is a facial version of an erection.

But although the route must not be confused with the destination, few travel unless they hope to arrive. The path typically lies through sex to love, which is the mature growth from the compost of passion, and that explains why St Valentine's Day presents tend more to the lingerie than (say) the cutlery end of things, for whereas cutlery is an adjunct of the domestic arrangements associated with long-term affections, gifts of lingerie are part of the invitation thither.

For this reason also romance is regarded by prudes and moralists as the primrose path to perdition. In the austere days of republican Rome, Cato the Censor expelled Lucius Manilius from the Senate because he had kissed his wife in public. Cato would have felt at home in the explosion of chastity that gripped nascent Christianity six centuries later, around AD 400. Recognising that female beauty is the most powerful drug in the world, male theologians then, as so many beforehand among the Jews and since then among the Muslims, sought to nip the bud of romance by requiring women to disguise the lubricious summons, endowed upon them by biology, in the flow of their hair and curve of their hips, by hiding these things beneath veils and shapeless robes.

These life-denying ordinances – which in the view of some insult not only all men and women but nature itself – have a mighty enemy in art. From Titian to Renoir the beauty of flesh and its clarion call to the successive heights of romance, passion, coition and fruition, are magnificently captured. In the secular songs of England's supreme composer, Henry Purcell, with their haunting jazz-like cadences and dissonances, romance is given its consummate aural shape. Purcell had a genius, never matched, for fitting English words to music, and in the song that is arguably the greatest ever written, 'O Fair Cedaria', he makes romance and desire liquefy and float as palpably to the ear as love itself to the heart.

In the calendar of the Catholic Church there are three St Valentines, two of them buried under the Flaminian Way outside Rome and the third in Africa. That is all that is known of them, except that their collective feast day is 14 February. In the Middle Ages the fact that birds begin to pair in mid-February gave rise to an association between St Valentine's Day and courtship. Chaucer's Parliament of Fowls has the lines, 'For this was on seynt Valentyne's day, / Whan every foul cometh there to chese his make [mate] . . .' In the Paston Letters Dame Elizabeth Brews, writing to John Paston to encourage his wooing of her daughter, says, 'And, cousin mine, upon Monday is Saint Valentine's Day and every bird chooses himself a mate, and if it like you to come on Thursday night, and make provision that you may abide till then, I trust to God that ye shall speak to my husband and I shall pray that we may bring the matter to a conclusion.' (Her match-making worked.)

According to Oscar Wilde, romance is deception: first of oneself, subsequently of others. Kinder observers say it involves the lesser evil of illusion. Suppose it does: yet romantic illusions add colour to reality's monochrome, and enliven hope; and have to be a good and welcome thing therefore.

Love

According to the great romantic conspiracy of modern times, there is a state of mind in which one adult human being regards another with a particular mixture of regard, tenderness, respect, desire, concern, affection and possessiveness, and this state of mind is a permanent or at least semi-permanent one which is very pleasant to be in, and, blissful when reciprocated. It is called 'love', and in this utopian guise is premised in a million novels and films, and is mistakenly believed to be one of the great goals and goods of the human condition.

The truth is that what people think of as love is a blind biological mechanism for initiating a new generation of human genes and protecting their carriers in their vulnerable early years. It falls into phases of unequal length: a short phase of sexual infatuation, and a long phase of habit and inertia. The infatuation phase sees much exchanging of saliva, sperm and body gases, each with their individual character and freight of microbes and viruses, and this (in the biological default case of a heterosexual pairing) might do more than merely prepare the female partner's immune system to tolerate a possible foetus with its foreign DNA; it might also induce a subtle form of addiction in both partners, which keeps them together during the habit stage that follows close behind.

Cynical? Alas, merely true. There is indeed such a thing as love, and it indeed involves tenderness, concern, affection and regard, though not perhaps the desire and possessiveness which are the attributes of infatuation. This love is what one feels for parents (sometimes), children and friends – and note that one's marital partner might become a friend too, and thus qualify. But whatever name is best appropriate to the youth of a relationship, in which greedy sex is had in lifts and cars, and the parties cannot bear to be apart, it is not love. And likewise, whatever name is best appropriate to the reason why a couple stick together through routines of domestic life, moving groceries and children about at frequent intervals and watching too much television, it is not love.

The first phase is a species of frenzy. The ancient Greeks feared it, as a punishment from the gods, and preferred cool reason to the rages of passion. The second phase is a species of intermittent anaesthesia, in which numbness makes almost bearable the anxious boredom of parenthood, and the tensions, provocations and annoyances of living squashed against another person year after year in a small space. They say a cat needs an acre of territory, so all urban cats are in a neurasthenic condition; pity, then, the poor human being whose acre has been sacrificed to 'love'.

On the other hand, some achieve love in the mythical sense of the romances, by turning their infatuation phase, in a somewhat lower and therefore more sustainable key, into a permanent state. The secret? Always making time for imaginatively good sex.

Desire

According to George Bernard Shaw, life's two keenest tragedies are: not getting what you desire, and getting what you desire. Because it must also be a tragedy not to desire anything, given that desiring is the mark of being alive, humankind seems to be in a bind.

Buddhists certainly think so. They believe that desire anchors us to illusion and suffering. 'Desire is the supreme disease,' says the Dhammapada; 'from desire rises sorrow.' Overcoming desire is a condition of release from reincarnation. This idea is not confined to Eastern asceticism. The Desert Fathers and the self-castrating martyrs of the early Church took an even harsher view: for them desire is the route not merely to sorrow but to damnation. It will surprise some to learn that classical Epicureanism, the philosophy that enjoins the pursuit of pleasure and the avoidance of pain, also frowned on desire, arguing that it invariably contains the seeds of pain. Pleasure for its founder Epicurus consisted in sipping water and eating morsels of bread in the shade of a tree, talking with friends. Modern Epicureans think that pleasure consists in the satisfaction of desires, and when they suffer as a result they are apt to agree, for a while, with their ancient forebears.

The usual consequence for those who seek to root out all desire is the inflation of small desires into mountainous ones. More moderate – because more realistic, perhaps – moralists preach continence instead, asking for desire to be not expunged, but managed and directed – by which they mean, diminished.

Are these dampening views right? An answer requires drawing

a three-way distinction among desires, needs and interests. If you desire something you naturally think you need it, although that is not inevitably or even frequently the case. People can sometimes be unaware of their needs, just as they can be unaware of what is in their best interests. Sometimes people might specifically not desire to fulfil a need – for example, to visit the dentist. But there cannot be such a thing as an unrecognised desire, any more than there can be unfelt pains or silent noises. This is because desire is pre-eminently a conscious, obvious, insistent state, hard to ignore and sometimes impossible to resist. And we often desire exactly what we do not need, and even what we should not need – as for example that extra piece of cake, that exorbitantly expensive necklace, our neighbour's wife.

Grant all this, yet recall that without desire there would be no humanity. Desire is nature's instrument of self-perpetuation. Cynics say that no fully rational individual would fall in love, still less marry, even less again have children. The power of desire, superior by far to that of reason, ensures that even the genes of cynics continue down the generations. Accepting this is a kind of liberation; but in licensing desire it does not thereby invalidate the claims of rationality. Perhaps one should, for the greater good, desire a balance between them.

Marriage

When San Francisco's mayor permitted a spate of gay marriages he initiated a predictable chain of events: America's moral traditionalists had a hold on the political party then running Washington, and they used it to prompt the President of the republic himself to seek a constitutional amendment entrenching heterosexual monogamous marriage, which he hyperbolically described as 'the most fundamental institution of civilisation'.

The source of the confusions that consequently multiplied in America's matrimonial debate was the conflation of two separate meanings of the word 'marriage'. The confusions are typically deepened by the usual lack of historical and cultural knowledge about the variety in humanity's domestic arrangements, even in the Western Judaeo-Christian tradition which moralists assume to be carved in stone, and which is not.

In its primary sense, marriage denotes a long-term committed relationship between people who pool their resources and endeavours and share the consequences, both good and bad. The arrangement turns on divisions of labour, and because children in most parts of the world and history are economic assets, it has centrally involved producing and raising as many as possible.

Again in most parts of the world and history, marriage in this sense has been based on utility, dynasty, and tribal or property considerations, and rarely on the untrustworthy basis of youthful emotions or passing fancies. Yet again, very few societies have restricted marriage to monogamy; there is even at least one where women take several husbands.

In this great sociological and historical bulk of marriage the central point has therefore always been on the commitment of people (two or more) to live together with a view to sharing life's demands and gifts, and producing and raising the next generation. This is marriage in the true sense, and it is focally about the nature of a relationship. In most societies such relationships receive social recognition and support, and are regulated by ceremony and tradition. The manner in which social recognition is accorded varies widely, but the point is the same.

The other sense of marriage is a three-way legal contract between two people and the state, giving the state a jurisdiction in the relationship when it goes wrong, which means a right to dispose of the joint obligations and property of the other two parties. Marriage as a legal institution has its present form in Western countries as a result of medieval concerns over property and inheritance rights. Its main point was control of women: female chastity and severe penalties for its absence ensured that men could be reasonably confident about leaving their property to their own offspring. (Only the wealthy, therefore, used to marry contractually.) In England the way this legal institution is put into effect has been regulated into a single form only since the eighteenth century, when general wealth had spread more widely and more people had property to pass to inheritors. Prior to that there were many ways to get married in the first sense, including the age-old one that held sway in the early Christian Church: simply by living together.

Everyone accepts that the mutual benefits of living in a committed relationship are great, and that human happiness and flourishing is best served by doing so. Whenever and wherever they occur, therefore, they are a cause of celebration. Or rather: except where narrow, ignorant and ungenerous views of what is acceptable in human relationships excludes all but monogamous heterosexuals from the great good that mutual affections and shared lives offer.

Gay couples in San Francisco flocked to get married in the second sense of the term (they were of course already married in the first sense) when the opportunity came, because they were hungry for the social recognition which they suppose that the second sense of marriage now represents. But this of course is what moral conservatives explicitly wish to deny them. To their chagrin, moral conservatives cannot prevent people loving each other, living together and helping and comforting each other in their daily lives; but they can mean-spiritedly withhold the blessing and support of the community for doing it.

Moral conservatives say that non-heterosexual relationships are 'unnatural' because they are not focused on producing children (which, some further add, is the only justification for sex). Thanks to the kindness of science, it is no longer true that same-sex couples cannot have children. What children need is love and nurture, not limitations on who is allowed to provide it; heterosexuality is not a necessity for parenthood.

Moreover, if having children is the centrepiece in conservative views of marriage, polygamy is the logical choice wherever women outnumber men. Perhaps this is the constitutional amendment the US President should really have sought.

Monogamy

In its original meaning 'monogamy' meant the practice of marrying only once in a lifetime (the word derived from ancient Greek *monos*, meaning 'one' and *gamos*, meaning 'to marry'.) Its two main modern meanings are rather different: one is the state or custom of being married to one person at a time, the other is the condition or practice of having a single mate during a given period. This latter is the zoological sense in which bearded experts talk of birds being monogamous; it was once believed that 90 per cent of all avian species are such, but it is now known that although a female bird might choose a single male to help her build a nest and feed the chicks, she – while he is off collecting twigs – is more often than not off collecting sperm from other males.

And so it is with most species – and with most of mankind. Ethologists tell us that only 1 to 2 per cent of all species are monogamous in the zoological sense. None of the simian species are so; the singular appearance of monogamy among orang-utans has more to do with their obesity and idleness than with their uniqueness. Our close relatives, the chimpanzees, practise a form of group marriage; our very closest relatives, the bonobos, indulge in indiscriminate and perpetual orgy. Among the 850 or so human societies recognised by anthropology, 83 per cent practise polygyny (in which a man has more than one wife); monogamy is the official social norm in only 16 per cent of human societies, in the sense that people have one socially recognised main partner at a time. But in every one of these societies, other more and less transient relationships of a sexual, or both an emotional and sexual, kind are the norm for the majority of people, not just in one-night stands at office parties, 'affairs' and the keeping of mistresses, but in institutional terms too, in the practice of prostitution, which is a very ancient and indispensable prop to the social order – and especially to monogamy in those few societies which theoretically claim to practise it.

As the tenor of these last remarks suggests, monogamy has practically speaking never existed anywhere at any time, except in the restricted and irrelevant original Greek sense in which a person might marry (i.e. go through a marriage ceremony) only once in a lifetime, whatever else he or she had in the way of relationships either sexual, or sexual and emotional, at various times of life. Two factors explain the non-existence in practical terms of monogamy in the modern sense – that is, as the committed relationship intended to be long-term, forsaking all others. One is that most people have more than one such partner during the course of their lives, even if non-simultaneously, and therefore they can be counted as monogamous only for the time that they are in a given relationship while not having other such partners. Strictly speaking, they are polygamous, but serially rather than synchronically: the multiple partners come in separated succession, not in groups.

But secondly, the best sociological researches show that about 40 per cent of women in long-term relationships have affairs with other partners, and about 70 per cent of men (this excludes one-night stands and visits to prostitutes). Given that some of the infidels are in relationships with non-infidels, it follows that over 80 per cent of all long-term committed relationships are touched by 'unfaithfulness' at some point. However one describes them, they are therefore not genuinely monogamous.

What these facts and figures baldly announce is that human beings are not naturally monogamous creatures, any more than the other 98 per cent of creatures in the zoological realm. Most

societies traditionally recognised this and arranged their institutions accordingly. Of these most appear to have done so to
the great advantage of men; there is only one currently known
polyandrous society, in the foothills of the Himalayas, where
women marry all the brothers from the same family. Happily
for them the younger brothers are expected to go with the herds
into the upper pastures for part of the year. But one can see
some advantages for these women in having a plurality of males
at their disposal.

It is scarcely needful to point out the advantages to men of
polygyny, providing that domestic peace is the norm in the
harem. Whether or not it is a male conspiracy to appeal to
sociobiology to explain the greater propensity towards multiple
partners displayed by men – the usual story tells us that they
are genetically determined to broadcast their seed as widely as
possible – it is certainly the case that in the rest of nature
females are not shy about seeking the best sperm on the market.
Recent studies show that it is not only female discernment
in inspecting gaudy male mating displays that does this, but
magnificent promiscuity, and even intrauterine selection of the
healthiest sperm.

The conclusion to be drawn from all the foregoing is that
monogamy is not natural, if nature is the model to follow, nor
historical, if lessons are to be learned from history and sociology.
(And where else might our models and lessons come from?) It
remains only to ask whether, in the face of such evidence,
monogamy is nevertheless desirable. Votaries of the ethics, such
as they are, of the Judaeo-Christian tradition are keen to claim
that their view of human relationships constitutes an ascent
over all other forms. They claim, remember, that the only good
kind of relationship involving sex is one in which a pair of
otherwise wholly inexperienced members of both sexes should
come together and exclusively thereafter own and control one
another's sexual expression and needs. This wise, humane and
perceptive prescript has either in fact or in tendency loaded the

world with such suffering, such frustration, so much sorrow, and so many lies and broken hearts, that it has to be considered a work of evil genius. The fact that in practice humanity has raised two fingers at it as an ideal of life is no surprise at all. And that answers the question of whether monogamy (as the Judaeo-Christian ideal sees it) is desirable despite being unnatural and unhistorical.

How many readers of these words has had only one sexual partner? How many have been faithful during the course of every (note: *every*) relationship they have had? Suppose you have been married for twenty years and never once in that time 'cheated' on your spouse. Still, did you have lovers before then? If, which heaven forfend, your partner were to die or leave, would you not hope to start another relationship at some point? A single 'yes' to any of these questions makes you a polygamist, in the real meaning of the term. And a good thing too.

Those five last words are best not misconstrued. Polygamy – or let us call it non-monogamy, as a more general and neutral term, meaning 'having more than one partner during the course of a life' – is good because it widens and deepens experience in an area whose health is essential to the life well lived. It might mean having more than one simultaneous partner, but it need not, and quite often it is better not. Until people have learned not to entangle their domestic projects – home building, having children – with their sexual affinities, with the result that interruptions of the latter typically mean destruction of the former, it might even be better to restrict synchronicities to very limited periods, if at all; as for example when a new relationship supersedes an old one (an inevitability when couples who started together when young have since grown apart: older and wiser couples make stronger bonds). There is good reason to suspect that the best kinds of sexual and emotional relationships are those in which there is sufficient mutuality and exclusivity to allow deep understanding to evolve; how often people utter the cliché, no less profoundly true for being one, that the best sex is the sex you have with the one you really love. And this implies that the best relationships are post-polygamous monogamies voluntarily chosen by those in them.

Friendship

Friendship is a single soul dwelling in two bodies.

ARISTOTLE

It is a universal truth that there are at least two views on any subject (which suggests that one should now say, 'Or perhaps not?'). This is why it is possible to note that friendship is treated by the philosophical tradition as a central good, and yet so courteous a philosopher as Confucius can say, 'No one really minds seeing a friend fall off a roof.'

If Confucius is right, the philosophical tradition has got something wrong. But on this particular matter it has arguably got things right. Therefore (by the deductive form known as *modus tollens*) Confucius should only have said 'some people do not mind'.

Here is why. Human beings are essentially social animals, 'essentially' meaning 'that which crucially defines'. Relationships are vital not just to the well-being but to the identity of all but the oddest individuals. Our intimate relationships are few in number (restricted as they are to family and lovers) and idiosyncratic in character, and play a rather odd though deep role in making us what we are. But friendships have the majority influence in determining the shape of our social personae, especially in the formative period between the second and fourth decades of our lives; and therefore one good way to know what sort of person someone really is, is to examine not the friends but the friendships he has maintained through time.

There are different ways of expressing the point that friendships form us, most familiarly perhaps by invoking the idea of peer influence, which in turn is most obvious in adolescence. (Educational psychologists say that males are adolescent until aged thirty, females until twenty. The ancient Greeks agreed with the first part of this thesis, setting male coming-of-age at thirty; their women were kept locked in permanent political and social minority.) But it is important not to restrict the idea of friendship to current living humans, despite this being the majority category for all of us. For one can have friendships with writers dead and gone, the characters in their books, historical figures, even (after a fashion) with cats, dogs and horses.

The key lies in who we talk to, and who we listen to, on what really concerns us. We can sometimes talk more honestly to strangers than to friends, but not with the same degree of significance, because what we discuss with friends stays alive in the relationship thereafter, affecting its course and influencing the character of the parties to it. Aristotle described a friend as 'another self', and that is sometimes true enough to make a friend the deceiver we need when we need to be deceived, and the absolver we need when we need absolution. But more importantly still, friends are the Others we need, and who need us, for the sake of the difference and connectedness which give us the feedback, the testing ground, the support and the acceptably modulated challenges that condition us – and the companionship and merriment that keep us sane.

In a world full of enmity it is always interesting to contemplate the nature of friendship. Received wisdom has it that a friend is a person who gives without being asked; who understands, or tries to; who rejoices at good fortune and supports through bad; who tells unpleasant truths and pleasant untruths when either is necessary; whose affection is freely given, and who makes the innocent and proper assumption that all the claims, expectations, rights and duties of this vital and valuable human bond are reciprocal.

Who could disagree? Perhaps the most important human relationship is the parenting, and especially mothering, of small children. But even the latter has friendship as part of its goal, if successful. Because friends are independent partners in their relationship, achieving friendship with one's offspring means that the project of helping them grow into freedom has worked.

The great philosopher of friendship is Aristotle. In two striking chapters of his *Nicomachean Ethics* he distinguishes genuine friendship from two simulacra, one in which the basis of the relationship is pleasure, the other in which it is mutual usefulness. These shallow forms of friendship last only as long as the pleasure or utility they afford, says Aristotle, whereas true friendship lasts because it is 'grounded in good', in the sense that one wishes for one's friend what is best for him. Aristotle calls this friendship 'perfected' or 'completed' because its goal lies wholly within the relationship itself, and does not treat it as merely instrumental for some other or further end.

When Aristotle says that a friend is 'another self', he means that the kind of concern one properly has for one's own good is extended to one's friend too. Proper self-concern is appropriate for an ethical individual, who will be motivated thereby to act nobly, and to make intelligent decisions about how to choose and act – and who will therefore always see that, as a social being, what is best for himself is at one with what is best for his friends and (ultimately) community. To treat a friend as another self, therefore, is always to will the best for him for his own sake.

The Aristotelian ideal of friendship is personal and mutual, and the very highest friendships are exclusive. Other philosophers took a different view. Immanuel Kant held that the truly virtuous individual will offer friendship to all other people equally, and that it is legitimate for people to expect a reciprocity of pleasure and utility. Søren Kierkegaard rejected Aristotle's view on the Christian ground that since one is to love all one's neighbours, there is no room for friendships that exclude any of them or discriminate among them.

These opinions are not, as it happens, inconsistent with Aristotle's view. One can nourish benevolent feelings towards the rest of humanity in general, and work for its good – and can appropriately expect from most of one's acquaintanceships a mutuality of pleasure and usefulness – while at the same time enjoying true friendship, in Aristotle's sense, with just one or some others. The key is that the overriding point of the relationship is the relationship itself. How indeed could one be a genuinely good friend to one's lover, one's family, one's chosen comrades, without offering them more of oneself than to strangers, however much one is concerned to be a responsible part of the comity of man? For friendship is by its nature particular, with its focus in individual things, in confidences and the security provided by mutual understanding. Multiplying such relationships too far makes each one less.

'The friends thou hast, and their adoption tried,' said Polonius, 'Grapple them to thy soul with hoops of steel; / But do not dull thy palm with entertainment / Of each new-hatched, unfledged comrade.' This advice seems to render the making of new friends impossible, and therefore needs qualification; but it suggests an allied truth, which is that friendships, once made, need tending; and nothing replaces time together, in circumstances where other pressures are lifted so that the gates of communication can spring open, allowing free trade to pass between.

Infidelity

Are you guilty of infidelity if you have an internet flirtation with someone other than the person you have a real-life relationship with? Most people polled on the subject answer in the affirmative, with more women than men believing it is likely to damage real-life relationships.

Another form of infidelity is censorship of news, such as occurs in totalitarian countries like China and North Korea. It is infidelity to the people of such countries, whose governments cannot trust the population with accurate reporting of points of view other than those sanitised for the protection of their unelected leaders.

Public and private infidelities are different things, and work their harm on different scales. But they share a number of common features, chiefly the breach of trust which, implicitly or explicitly, underlies every relationship, whether of person to person, government to people, employee to employer and vice versa. When the basis of a relationship is explicit, as when a contract is in force, it is clear what constitutes a breach; but many contracts, especially between private individuals, are unvoiced and inexplicit, resting on assumptions about the duties and mutually acceptable boundary conditions involved.

In considering whether virtual, and therefore perforce verbal, dalliance with a stranger by electronic means is a form of infidelity, it has to be remembered that many such e-relationships involve explicit sexual exchanges, and some flirters form a dependence on their correspondents. Of course if such exchanges result in actual meetings and physical affairs (and many do), the question answers itself. But if they stay in cyber-space, is it not merely an imitation of infidelity, as much a simulacrum as the sex involved?

Some of cyber-flirting's defenders claim that it provides a safety valve which protects actual relationships from the real thing. Others add that it is merely an extension of such ephemeral and harmless activities as looking at an attractive stranger across the street, or indulging a sexual fantasy during intimacy with a partner. Critics of the practice, however, insist that infidelity is a psychological matter much more than a physical one, and that it is what is said and shared, and not the medium that conveys either, which is the crucial point.

But: remember the poignant film *Brief Encounter*? Interestingly, its very point is that Laura Jesson (memorably played by Celia Johnson) was not after all unfaithful to her husband, though what she and Dr Alec Harvey (equally memorably played by Trevor Howard) felt and did was a lot more than most internet flirters do. That film appeared in 1945 when many people must have wondered what their partners did – what encounters brief and otherwise they engaged in – during the years of wartime separation. All things then happened in real time and space; you might say, in virtually a different world. The question is: has the internet so changed the rules that what was once not infidelity has become so as a result?

Cheating

Man is practised in disguise; he cheats the most discerning eyes.
GAY

According to Blaise Pascal, 'mutual cheating is the foundation of society'. Research published by two Swiss social scientists* shows, happily, that he is wrong. Their investigations reveal that people are more willing to help others than to cheat them, even when the cost to themselves is great; and they are quick to punish cheating when they detect it, even when they are not themselves its victims.

The Swiss researchers found, in short, that people are surprisingly selfless. To act in the interests of others without reward is the definition of altruism. It might come as news to many that altruism is commonplace. But, as the researchers correctly pointed out, society could not get along without it.

These observations suggest that the self-sacrifice of soldiers and rescue workers, and of all those everywhere in history who supererogated on behalf of others, is a defining mark of the social instinct in mankind. Society depends upon a large measure of

---

* In an article titled 'Altruistic Punishment in Humans', which appeared in the journal *Nature*, Ernst Fehr of the University of Zurich and Simon Gachter of the University of St Gallen in Switzerland offer evidence that people will seek to punish a cheat even when the punishment is costly to themselves and offers no material benefit – the very definition of altruism. The researchers propose that the threat of such punishment may have been crucial to the evolution of human civilisation.

mutual trust and assistance, on co-operation with others who are not immediate kin, and on preparedness to share, to sympathise, to give and to protect. The media are quick to report conflict and hatred; it is usually only in passing that they mention the far greater presence of co-operation in the world. Suppose a gunman shoots someone; many other people involved in such an incident – in the ambulance service, the local hospital, the police, the government, society at large – either help in trying to save the victim, or condemn the ugly cheating of life and peace which is the stock-in-trade of violent people (almost always men). It might appear that sentiment is worth little in the face of bullets; but the fact is that most places and most people are peaceful precisely because the reverse is true.

The Swiss researchers found that large majorities of people in their sample groups became angry when they encountered cheating and injustice, even when they were detached observers of it. The finding is supported by anthropologists who note that in egalitarian hunter-gatherer societies fairness matters greatly because survival depends upon it, and therefore that transgressions of the rules are harshly punished. The same impulses – reflecting the same truth, in more complicated and indirect ways – survive in advanced societies. Indeed they survive the more strongly because market versions of such societies are structured on principles which cheating undermines and sometimes destroys.

If the crucial term in the above quotation from Pascal is translated differently, as 'deception' rather than 'cheating', he can be construed as advancing a different point, namely that society depends for its effectiveness on mild forms of mutual deception, functioning as a social lubricant. It is certainly true that too much frankness about minor things, such as one's view of others' hair-styles or dress sense, is not conducive to harmony. In the normal round, a degree of assumed bonhomie generates more good, or at least less harm, than the frank manifestation of dislike or disapproval. Trying to vindicate the latter by calling it 'honesty' will not do; the truly honest name for such behaviour is boorishness.

Constructive mutual deceptions readily enough degenerate into hypocrisy, though, and sometimes the dividing line is invisible. But, as Dr Johnson remarked, 'The truth is, there is very little hypocrisy in the world,' despite our insistent belief to the contrary; and the reason is that hypocrisy is either occasional or habitual – and if it is the latter, it has become the man himself and is hypocrisy no longer.

Cynics expect us all to cheat at times, and like to describe even our kindly attempts at social pleasantry as deceit. But their deeper belief is that the worst kind of 'deep design and deceit malign' is the real basis of society, snaring us together in mutual exploitation. 'Without dissimulation, no business could be carried on,' Chesterfield told his son; and legion are those who agree. To them, therefore, the Swiss research is a cheering and hopeful riposte.

Parting

Partings might be endings, or new beginnings; they might be too temporary for the sweet sorrow they are poetically identified with, or – as always in the case of a collapsed domestic arrangement where one party has not yet finished being in love – they might leave wounds that either take too long to heal, or never do.

The idea of a parting of the ways (in the literal sense of a fork in the road) offers the following conundrum. You come to the parting, and do not know which road to take in order to reach your destination. Two people are stationed there, and you know that one is consistently veracious, the other an invariable liar. You do not know which is which, yet you are allowed only one question. What do you ask?

No matter what the circumstances, to part from anything of value, whether people or things, places or occupations, is to forfeit something of oneself. It is as if the other entity has grown into one, sending a tentacle under the skin, suggesting the reason for describing oneself as attached to it. In a frozen-food warehouse once I saw a workman leave the palm print of his hand on the surface of a box; he had made the mistake of taking off his glove. In 'Rondel de l'adieu' Edmond Haraucourt expresses the metaphorical version of this, associating it with the Schopenhauerian idea of thereby tasting a fraction of mortality, in a verse from which a well-known song takes a line: 'To leave is to die a little; / It is to die to what one loves; / One leaves behind a little of oneself / At any hour, any place.'

A test of Bruno Bettelheim's view that fairy tales offer children preparations for life – seeing parental death, or perhaps just adulthood, allegorised in Hansel's and Gretel's abandonment in a wood; and, obviously, sexual awakening in the Prince's buss on Sleeping Beauty's lips – would be to see how many of them concern partings. Both of these are about partings (from child-hood, from innocence), and since every progression through life is a parting from what went before, they are a good augury that Bettelheim's thesis stands up. Such canticles of parting teach that to gain you have to give up, that to be alive is to change, and that change involves the death of things so that they can become the past. Consider the tale of the Seven Ravens, who are brothers metamorphosed by a curse, whose sister leaves home to look for them and cuts off a finger to serve as a key to unlock the door of the Glass Mountain where they are impris-oned. In this tale a sequence of partings makes a homecoming – which no doubt all the best do.

André Gide was of the optimistic tendency which sees a fresh start in every parting, while a more sardonic Italian proverb has it that too many starts make for few endings. In fact, rather few partings are endings, despite the truth in the opening flourish above; when Ruskin wrote, 'God alone can finish,' he was not being pious, but succinct: paintings, like poems, are never fin-ished, only abandoned, so when the maker of them parts from them, it is not because they have come to an end, but because more than half of all art is knowing when to stop.

The answer to the conundrum of the forked road is: you ask one of the men (it does not matter which) to point out the road that the other man would say is your route. And then, since the pointed-out road will be the wrong one, you take the other road. For the liar will lie about which road the truth-teller would indicate, and the truth-teller will indicate the liar's choice; so both will point at the wrong road. This happily mimics life: the right road is usually clear to anyone who will give some thought to the puzzle of which, among so many wrong roads, is the right one, for truth and falsehood combine to give truth whenever ways reach a parting.

Nudity

Man is the only animal whose nudity offends his companions.
MONTAIGNE

In the early summer of 1885 a heated correspondence broke out in *The Times* as a result of a letter from 'A British Matron', writing to say that she had been to an exhibition at which paintings of nudes had been 'flaunted before the public', obliging viewers to 'turn from them in disgust because their sense of decency was revolted by them'.

Anyone who turned in disgust from this matron, revolted by her attitude, might thereby be defending the view of one of her opponents in the debate, who diagnosed her attitude as a failure of taste. For him the human form was the most beautiful shape in nature, and he rejoiced that the artists of his day were celebrating it.

It is itself a matter of taste whether the human form – at least, in its respectively athletic and nubile manifestations as young adult males and females – is nature's loveliest shape, for there is much competition elsewhere; and anyway beauty has many guises, each its own kind, which it is pointless to rank. Most human shapes are not especially beautiful, even if they are otherwise interesting or amusing; and only prudery makes nakedness a matter of sexual offence. Naturists say that there is nothing in the slightest erotomaniac about their hobby, and in light of the plasticities, protuberances and pendulosities of the average human body, they can well be believed.

It is likely that the British Matron was offended not merely by the undraped shapes she saw in the 1885 exhibition, most of them female, but by the simmering eroticism they expressed. In the glowing and technically superlative paintings of Lord Leighton and Lawrence Alma-Tadema there is palpable aphrodisiac sentiment, in which the languor and heat of spread limbs, the sultry atmosphere of Oriental slave-markets, the phosphorescent milkiness of breasts and necks, speak directly to the sexual interest of the viewer. These artists were frankly interested in depicting sexual beauty, and hostile critics attack them on the grounds that their works are voyeuristic, masquerading as high art in order to cloak mere pandering to the indecency and exploitation of the male gaze.

Whereas English painters contemporary with the British Matron are only now getting their due, having been damned for their sentimentality as well as their voyeurism – and for painting with such photographic clarity as to offend the sensibilities of the aesthetes who turned Impressionism into a billion-dollar business – their French forerunners (such as the eighteenth century's François Boucher) had long since established the celebration of the erotically beautiful, and of course without demur in their own land. When Sophie Dahl controversially appeared in a perfume advertisement, her pose was Boucher's 'L'Odalisca' in reverse – far more decorous than the original, as it happens, perhaps because hearts beat fainter nowadays, at least in the Advertising Standards Authority, fearful of the two dozen or so British Matrons (of both sexes) who regularly write to them.

The world of classical antiquity agreed with the British Matron's 1885 opponent. The healthy, fit, trained male body seemed the imago of perfection to the ancients, and its beauty was a matter of moral significance as well as visual delight. Proportion, harmony and poise expressed man's role as the measure of things. The idea of the free movement of limbs in running and wrestling, of fleetness and suppleness, of grace in acts of throwing the discus or riding a horse, brought intellectual as well as sensual pleasure. The word 'gymnasium' comes from *gymnos*, meaning 'naked', and denotes the place where the virtues of physical beauty were cultivated.

Both the Greeks and the Romans enjoyed female beauty too, and respected its power of sexual beguilement, which a senior and much-celebrated goddess represented. But for their domestic concern of having children – a key security – their honours were paid to just part of the naked human form: the phallus, depicted in inseminatingly alert form in public squares, on every house-front, at every crossroads, and in lucky amulets worn on girls' arms. To step along any street of ancient Rome would inflame the cheeks of British Matrons of all epochs – whose shame should therefore be for themselves.

Pleasure

Has pleasure become one of the lost arts of civilisation? It might be natural to think so, when one considers how many priestly centuries have been devoted to teaching people to avoid it, and when one sees how far, in these otherwise happily more sceptical times, it has been replaced by a raft of substitutes, most of them electronically produced. But in fact so essential is pleasure to human existence that neither the capacity for feeling it nor the skill of inducing it has been quite lost, and both lie open to anyone who will give them thought.

The first rule of pleasure is to face the nay-sayers and stare them down. Death, according to the Upanishads, admonished mankind with the words: 'The good and the pleasant are two different things. Happy he who clings to the good; he who chooses pleasure has missed his goal.' This therefore is an old story – the Upanishads are among the earliest of scriptures – and it is a puzzle how it got started. Who first thought that life must be premised on denials if it is to be 'good'? Matters are so obviously the other way round. 'He has spent his life best who has enjoyed it most,' said the younger Samuel Butler, who believed that pleasure is a safer guide than hand-me-down notions of duty and rightness, and wrote a book to prove it.

The second rule of pleasure is simplicity. Complicating things in the hope of heightening, intensifying or prolonging pleasure carries the seeds of self-defeat. Think of an elaborate banquet, at which the sheer volume of dishes soon numbs the appetite. Or better, think of a long, expensive wedding, which subjects the invited to longueurs, artificial emotions, too much food and drink, uncomfortable clothes, an unhelpful mixture of generations, and false bonhomie, all in the pretence that a beautiful adventure has begun. Simplicity is the lesson taught by Epicurus, the ancient artist of pleasure, who knew that excess destroys its essence.

The third rule of pleasure is reciprocity. To find pleasure one must know how to give it, and that involves insight, sympathy and mutuality, all of them refinable virtues. Another way of putting the point is to say: there can be little true pleasure in what harms others. This is why Oscar Wilde was right to reject the Golden Rule, for if your rule is that you must do to others as you would have them do to you, then you make your own tastes a standard, and ignore the difference – and thus the real needs and desires – of others.

The fourth rule of pleasure is: identify its possibilities, especially basic ones, such perhaps as drinking cool water after a thirsty walk, reading a good book, playing music, experiencing the answer given by willing skin to a lover's caress. On these rest the ability to recognise true pleasure, and to give and receive it with grace; for recognising it, and giving and receiving it with grace, are the necessary foundations of its art.

Reputation

Oscar Kokoschka, when aged eighty, said, 'If you last, you will see your reputation die three times.' If true, this is a modern phenomenon; for it was once the case that losing a reputation was a permanent condition, and not just for women. Reputation was thought to be the best part of personhood: one's body might die, but the regard in which one stands in others' eyes survives that contingency, and matters more. So says Cassio in Shakespeare's *Othello*: 'O! I have lost my reputation. I have lost the immortal part of myself, and what remains is bestial.'

As Cassio's case illustrates, reputations are often undeservedly lost, just as they can be unmeritedly acquired. The occurrence of either of course tells us little about their owners and more about the gullibility or malice of those who bestow them in the first place. Moreover, time has a peculiar effect on reputations, often enhancing them, because history is a magnifying glass, making the generals, philosophers, poets and courtesans of bygone ages seem braver, cleverer, more lyrical or more beautiful than any contemporary practitioner of their various arts can be.

Is reputation merely a measure of popular judgement? That would make it much like mere celebrity. In the contemporary world, a pair of mutually serving voracious appetites, in the form of television's need for matter to broadcast and the public's need for gossip-rich narratives, has inflated the phenomenon of celebrity to gargantuan proportions. A whole industry depends on it. Soap-opera stars become both fictional and real-life objects of interest. Magazines come into existence to feed parasitically upon the television series and the private lives of the stars involved. Stars' private lives become as convoluted and dramatic as the soap-opera plots they perform, at least partly because of the inquisitiveness and invasiveness that their fame invites from a press eager to satisfy the punters. It is a self-induced, self-gorging, self-destructive enterprise, a monster eating its own entrails – in public.

But with a few exceptions this kind of fame, in which a star is a transitory cipher for public attention rather than a real person, is not the same as reputation. Reputation is a larger thing, and it differs from mere celebrity in a vital respect. It takes either much doing or many doings to be won, though only one thing to be lost; whereas celebrity can be acquired in an instant, and can remain despite – even indeed because of – the loss of what merited it, if anything did.

What reputations are worth having? Not bad ones, of course. Would one wish to be reputed a great lover, and remembered as clever, funny or brave? Would one best like to live in the hearts of people who, with love, regret one's absence? Would one like to have found or done something that helps others live better, and who recall the fact with gratitude? The choice is one's own; for though the final judge of reputations is time, the chief maker of them is oneself.

Madness

Without madness there can be no sanity, not just in the sense that the ideas of sanity and madness need each other to have meaning, but because unless people can be mad now and then – even if only a little – they could never hope to be sane. Love, drink, drugs and going on holiday provide the usually sane with the refreshment of temporary insanity, which in moderation does them good. This explains why it has never been possible for tyrants and moralists to outlaw these things successfully (though not for want of trying).

But real madness is a burden at least, and often a tragedy, for sufferers and those close to them. Sometimes it threatens society too. For both reasons society has to pay it attention. The tormented need help, and lunatics cannot be permitted, for their sakes and ours, to drive buses or mind children. In earlier and different times, madness was tolerated and even venerated as a mark of connection with the divine. Now not even those who still believe in the divine see madness in this light. Just as modern motorways have no room for ox-carts or wandering pedestrians, so modern society has little place for lives and ways that are too eccentric.

What, then, is madness? We have learned from the likes of Laing and Foucault to question medical theories about mental normality and abnormality, and we know that there are many kinds and degrees of both. Moreover, history is full of redefinitions of madness and revised attitudes towards it, from enjoyment of the village idiot to intolerance and murder of him.

Foucault viewed madness as an artificial category invented

by those with the power to decide what counts as normal. Others – including the mainstream of contemporary medical science – regard madness as an objective phenomenon, consisting in life-disrupting inability to relate in appropriate ways to the physical and social environment. Some of the chemical mechanisms of brain function whose disturbance can cause such disruption are now well enough understood for there to be chemical remedies. This seems to weigh the argument the objectivists' way.

Of course, florid cases of psychotic delusion which pose risks to others, or depressive illness causing terrible misery to its sufferer, are hardly well described in Foucault's terms, as merely inconveniences to the powerful. On this score, Foucault is plainly wrong. But attempts like his to contest the categories of modern psychological medicine at least remind us of the positive moral and aesthetic role played by non-standard mental states throughout history. Visions and ecstasies, as gifts from the gods, were thought to offer wisdom and prophetic insight. Sometimes madness was seen as punishment, that is true; but just as often it served as the deep well from which creative possibilities are drawn. That is why the ancients drank fermented liquors or ate magic mushrooms: they did it for the glimpse of greater things that the ensuing lunacies provided. Today, simple escape from the prosaic serves some as just as good an excuse.

Cowardice

In Ambrose Bierce's celebrated definition, cowardice is thinking with your feet when facing danger. To more judicious minds, and depending on the kind of peril in question, thinking with your feet might simply be the best thing to do; it might be what has consolingly been called 'the better part of valour'. The question is: how does one tell the difference?

Everyone knows that a coward dies a thousand deaths before he dies. This is an important and complex truth, for it implies the debilitating effect of so much prospective mortality. It tells us that cowardice saps confidence, loses opportunities, lays waste to talents, multiplies miseries unnecessarily. The best course is to refuse to be afraid until fear is really required. A good example for many is dental treatment. It has been well said that no man is a philosopher at the dentist, and countless nights have been lost to sleep by the imagined shriek of the drill. Some prefer weeks of throbbings and halitosis to an hour under the pitiless dental light. Cowardice, thus, is irrational.

In navy jargon two centuries ago cowards were described as 'shy'. Since then the connotations of the latter word have changed completely. Every implication of cowardice is negative, but those who are shy, timid and unconfident invite compassion and even affection. The reasons lie deep in two different directions. For a long time before the civic roots of Western civilisation in the classical epoch, warrior virtues held sway: valour, endurance, strength, ferocity in battle. During long ages when male preparedness to fight and die was essential to a community's safety, one of the worst offences was shirking in the face of danger.

If proof were needed that contemporary notions of cowardice are a residue of these ancient masculine imperatives, one need only note that they are almost exclusively applied to men. There is scarcely ever talk of women as cowards, not just because they are generally brave but because it is a term of calibration that has little place outside male avocations.

Shyness and timidity are attributes of the young, the vulnerable, the hurt, the needy. To describe people as shy or (say) dogs as timid is to imply that they merit protection of one or another kind, most especially from any harshness of approach. Interestingly, what makes a person timid is a generalisation of what makes someone a coward at the dentist: fear of the occasion and what it involves. But whereas we think the coward should be able to do better, to feel and behave differently, we think the timid soul cannot help what he or she feels, and cannot justly be expected to bloom suddenly into confidence. As this suggests, cowardice implies a lack of the right kind of moral effort, whereas shyness and timidity imply psychological deficits which need our respect.

As with most of our natural and unreflective ways of thinking about emotions, these attitudinal differences capture something real. To the coward they suggest a strategy: cultivate a reputation for timidity instead.

Public Concerns

Reason

In the closing years of the eighteenth century Francisco de Goya made a series of etchings illustrating aspects of his contemporary world, and called them *Los Caprichos* (*The Caprices*, or *Follies*). He published them in volume form with accompanying texts expressing his liberal Enlightenment conviction that humanity is held back by chains of superstition and ignorance, and particularly by the religious and political factors that promote both.

Goya's *Los Caprichos* quickly became one of the most influential graphic works in the history of Western art. One of the etchings in particular has become a familiar image, both for the striking way it conveys its message and because it captures the dominating theme of *Los Caprichos* as a whole. It is a picture of a man slumped over his desk in sleep, his unconsciousness permitting a swarm of threatening night-flying creatures to emerge from the shadows around him. On the side of the desk facing the viewer Goya painted an explanatory inscription which reads: '*El sueno de la razon produce monstruos*' – 'The sleep of reason produces monsters.'

It is a commonplace that the world is ruled by unreason. It is easy to see the monsters that stalk abroad, created and fuelled by emotion alone, especially those of anger, resentment, intolerance, greed and fear. The workings of these things cost the human family a great deal, both in pain and money; for they demand armies, police forces, secret agents, guns, equipment, courtrooms, prisons, hospitals and graveyards, all in constantly increasing quantities.

Commonplaces are not guaranteed to be true merely because everyone believes them, but this one has the doubtful distinction of being absolutely so. Still, it is not the whole truth. The evidence that reason also rules is everywhere as ubiquitous, though less obvious, usually because it is taken for granted. Consider any of the hundreds of great cities in the Western world, whose water supplies, sewage systems, telephones, electricity, shops, supermarkets and schools function with predictable efficiency almost all the time. That is the outcome of forethought and planning, and of good management and maintenance, all of them offspring of reason.

Moreover, the appurtenances of modern life, highly technologised as they are, show the power of reason concretised as applied science. It is scarcely needful to list the devices which assist every aspect of our lives and work from the moment we rise in the morning until we sleep at night – a reasonable sleep this time, ameliorated and sometimes, if there are obstacles, abetted by the works of reason.

Reason has been constructively at work throughout human history. It can be seen in the archaeologists' trove of shaped flints and axeheads from before the dawn of memory, in the street plan of the ancient city of Mohenjo Daro, in the irrigation canals, animal husbandry, buildings and jewellery of dynastic Egypt, and supremely in the rational and liberal air of classical Greece, the seed from which the West sprang.

Cynics will say that reason is not intrinsically benign; it has, for example, been at work throughout the development of the spear into the guided missile. And of course they are right. A chilling demonstration of this is to be found in the gas chambers of Auschwitz, or the torture equipment at the Spilberk fortress of Brno, once the chief political prison of the Austro-Hungarian Empire, and scene of the autobiographical tales in Silvio Pellico's *My Prisons*. The devices there are beautifully engineered, and each comes with a booklet of instructions detailing the results of careful research into their uses.

But it is a mistake to use such facts, as current fashion does, to reject a Whiggish view of human progress. From dentistry and central heating to human rights and the rule of law, for every backward step caused by malign uses of reason, its benign uses prompt two steps forward. Misuse of reason might yet return the world to pre-technological night; plenty of religious zealots hunger for just such a result, and are happy to use the latest technology to effect it. But, so far, reason's triumph is that the life of today's average Westerner is infinitely better than his ancestors' lives, thanks to its richly various benign endeavours, and despite all that malign reason and unreason have done.

The danger lies in an implication of the word 'Westerner'. Two thirds of the world still lives under the historic government of unreason – of superstition, ignorance and the associated divisions, hostilities and negative emotions that fuel conflict – and Goya's etchings would need little modification to illustrate them.

Western reason should not fall asleep when contemplating this fact, for it might never again wake up.

Opinion

Antiquity's greatest gossip was Aulus Gellius, a grammarian and seeker after curiosities who lived in the second century AD. Like a magpie he collected every bright bit of information he could find, and like a magpie he chattered about them endlessly. The result is a fascinating miscellany known to posterity as the *Attic Nights*. He was indefatigable and indiscriminate in his interests, which ranged from questions about whether certain kinds of flute-playing can cure gout, to why avarice makes people effeminate, and from fine points of Latin grammar to enquiries about the variation in length of pregnancies. But historians have found his hodgepodge useful for the glimpses it gives of life and thought in his day; and in some cases his quotations are our only remaining evidence of lost ancient texts.

One of the snippets in the *Attic Nights* concerns the great orator Demosthenes. As a young man, Gellius tells us, Demosthenes attended the Academy in Athens to hear Plato's lectures. But one day he saw a great crowd of people hurrying by, so he followed them out of curiosity. It transpired that they were going to listen to the demagogue Callistratus, a powerful orator skilled at swaying public opinion any way he liked. So impressed was Demosthenes by this manifestation of the suasive arts that he gave up listening to Plato, and followed Callistratus instead.

'Demagogue' means 'leader of the people', and what enchanted Demosthenes was the power of rhetoric to take people wherever its exponent wished. Oratory was an important piece of political equipment from Demosthenes' day until fifty years ago. It was, for a signal example, one of Churchill's chief weapons as a wartime leader. Indeed at one point it was all that stood between Britain and disaster. The intimacy of television interviews soon killed old-fashioned oratory, even though the art's last practitioners, such as Michael Foot and Tony Benn, used the occasional upturned crate as a platform for its exercise – perhaps an exercise in nostalgia, given how things had changed.

Oratory has gone but demagoguery still exists in politics, advertising and the press. Its aim is not the dissemination of truth, but of opinion; and in the important realm of press commentary on politics its aim is to move attitudes for or against, and thereby to enable or disable policy. In the competition between politicians and press the latter has by far the upper hand: it has more voices, little accountability, and freedom from the difficulties of government.

When the press feels that politicians have done an injury to some part of its collective body, it reacts with ferocity and in concert, for it is jealous of its prerogatives. Opinion and its close cousin sentiment are matters of great importance in politics. Facts of course also matter – but usually, from the press's point of view, only if they are uncomfortable for the governing party, for in a democracy the natural relation between government and press is usually one of opposition. The press has the important task of keeping a hawk's eye on government doings, and of informing and educating the public about them. That is why press freedom matters.

But there is so fine a line between freedom and licence that generally speaking everyone ignores it. This is not necessarily a bad thing; except when things go too far, and there is confusion between reportage and opinion, so that under the pretence of telling us what is going on the press tries to make us accept its view of what is going on. It would help if news pages and opinion pages were kept apart in spirit as well as in the geography of pagination.

Had Demosthenes persisted with Plato's lectures he would have heard him say that opinion concerns what is local, temporary and imperfect, whereas truth concerns what is perfect, eternal and unchanging. On this definition there can be no truth in human affairs. But even if Plato is right, there can still be opinion well formed and strongly supported. Demosthenes and the demagogues did not care whether opinions were right, only whether they could influence; if that attitude infected our own times too deeply, it would be a crippling attack on the health of society.

Prevention and Cure

Middle age has been defined as what happens when a person's broad mind and narrow waist change places. Onlookers notice this unhappy rearrangement long before its subject does. He, straining his buttons in indignation at what the world has become since the palmy days when he could see his feet, regards himself as unchanged in his principles but disadvantaged by the retrograde motion of society. In too many cases indignation and blood pressure rise in tandem until the fatal day when subject and world jointly cease to exist, at least from the subject's point of view.

Plutarch, writing about health two thousand years ago, had the measure of apoplexy. Recognising that the downward curve of metabolism intersects with the rising curve of wealth and sedentariness to explain at least the waistline half of the equation, he counselled moderation in diet, and continued regular exercise. This advice is now a cliché of prophylaxis, but it is intriguing to find that in the midst of the bleeping, winking, polysyllabic, white-coated medical wizardries of today, the best advice for health still echoes that given by the ancients. Plutarch also counselled proper rest, and self-schooling in the art of knowing when to worry over one's problems and when to set them aside until needed. We think the modern world discovered stress, perhaps because we think the modern world created it; but Plutarch is there before us, and with the simple remedy to hand.

It is said that advice given free is rarely heeded. Similarly, advice is disdained in direct proportion to its simplicity.

Moderate diet, exercise, proper rest – surely these cannot compete with expensive gym equipment, costly supplements, weekends in a spa, electronic toners, personal trainers, and a dozen other wallet-slimming aids besides? Yet – to take a familiar example – every January, which ought to be renamed Detoxuary in honour of its new deity, so easy a recourse as walking further, eating less, and getting to bed betimes seems perfectly inadequate to the demands of self-mortification required to compensate for the excesses of the preceding holiday season. Or is it indiscretions at the office party people are punishing themselves for, achieving purgatory for the conscience by purgation of the body?

Prevention is one thing, cure another. Within living memory medical science was far better at counselling the former than effecting the latter. Now it is miraculously potent at curing and remedying. The story of modern medicine is a remarkable testament to human genius; where once all it had to offer was advice and the placebo effect of authority, it now averts death itself, as many of us can testify who long ago might otherwise have dissolved back into earth and air.

But prevention is still the key to health, a truism everyone knows and few act upon. In his essay 'On Keeping Well' Plutarch takes this for granted, discussing instead the obstacles faced by prevention. He astutely observes that it is not greed and laziness that begin the destruction of health – these are, rather, marks that such destruction is already under way – but the bad encouragement we give each other to overindulge when we socialise, as when lads gather at the pub and drink excessively, and when rich dinners are fed to guests. Plutarch was not against indulgence as a moral holiday; far from it. He counselled instead against indulgence becoming the norm.

And he pointed out that disease not only spoils our enterprises and hopes but, even more, our pleasures. Mistreating one's health by incontinence is therefore precisely the wrong choice even for the hedonist. 'Pleasures and enjoyments do not come in time of disease, or if they do, they yield only a small part of what they properly should,' he remarked, thinking of sex; and thinking of food, he quoted the saying of Prodicus that 'health is the most divine sauce for our viands, for who can enjoy even the choicest dishes when suffering debauch or nausea?' And he noted what remains as true now as it was then, that the healthiest food is usually the cheapest.

Plutarch concluded by observing that just as the Athenians only voted for peace when wearing black, so the only person who gives proper thought to health is the sick man. To sum up his case he repeated a saying widely quoted in the Hellenistic world, referring to the continence of the philosophical life and the habitual simplicity of its fare: 'Those who dine with Plato get on pleasantly the next day also.' The saying is worth bringing back into currency.

Indulgence

On the third day of Christmas, which is to say, the day after Boxing Day, when the remains of the turkey coldly furnish forth the lunch table, and accumulations of indulgence have begun to tell on digestive systems and consciences, who could possibly want a gift of three French hens? For one thing, Christmas sees poultry enough; for another, there is a real necessity for something rallying in the way of reflection on the question of overindulgence, given what has just passed and the fact that New Year's Eve impends.

So here are glad tidings, which are that indulgence – even overindulgence – is good for you. It might not be good for you physically, which is all that the doomsayers can think about at the festive season, for whom weight gained, livers damaged and arteries clogged are all that count; but it is definitely good for you morally. 'Moral' does not here refer to occurrences behind filing cabinets at office parties, but to the psychological effect of having a 'moral holiday' by lifting constraints and enjoying what counts at all other times as excess.

The wisdom of having moral holidays was recognised even by those austere and self-contained sages of antiquity, the Epicureans. Today an Epicurean is anyone who likes the fine things in life and liberally indulges in them all year round; but originally it meant the opposite. Epicurus taught that the happiest life is a simple life of restraint, devoted to learning and reflection, and his motto accordingly was: 'Moderation in all things.' But he also taught moderation in moderation, so he and his disciples now and then had a grand feast, as a refreshment for the soul.

Every tradition everywhere has done, and does, likewise. The ancient practices of fasting, which survive in Ramadan and notionally in Lent, were begun and ended by lavish festivals, the best contemporary example being Brazil's Mardi Gras – Fat Tuesday – marking a farewell to the flesh (which is what 'carnival' means) for the forty lean days supposed to follow. In Europe and North America feasts have come to be associated mainly with the dark parts of the year in November and December – to brighten them up, obviously, in both literal and psychological ways. These dark days are now the retail industry's most luminous annual moment.

The sentimental view of Christmas is older than the kitsch version of it imported by our Victorian ancestors from Biedermeier Germany. Thomas Tusser, sixteenth-century author of a book of husbandry, tells his readers: 'At Christmas, play and make good cheer, for Christmas comes but once a year,' thereby inventing a proverb and eventually a cliché. Those with a jaundiced view of the event's compulsory confinements and socialisings are of course grateful for its low frequency. But cynics among them can at least enjoy the deeply pagan symbolism of yule log, mistletoe and ivy.

There once were many more annual occasions of moral holiday. Apart from the opening and ending of fasts there were fêtes and markets, weddings, harvest festivals, All-Hallows, and cognate opportunities. Christmas itself was a far more riotous affair in England – until 1555, to be exact, when a law banned the wild, drunken and libidinous revels held under the auspices of the 'Lord of Misrule', appointed to ensure that the twelve days of Christmas constituted a single unforgettable party. Although the Church participated (their Lord of Misrule was a 'Boy Bishop') the tradition of a December debauch was much older; it came from the lost reaches of prehistory via the Romans – and in their case specifically the Saturnalia. For a week in which the shortest day (21 December) was the exact centre, the Roman world was turned upside down: masters served servants, and everyone ate and drank themselves into a stupor.

The psychology behind such moral holidays is clearly astute. But their value lies not just in flexing what might otherwise be the unbendable bough. Excess teaches lessons; interesting and informative things are said and done, educative contrasts with sober times offer themselves, insights are gleaned. By some alchemy, Christmas is a better opportunity for these lessons even than the other occasions when families gather in the presence of alcohol, such as weddings and major anniversaries, doubtless because it goes on longer. What it comes down to is recognising that the hangover, the attack of indigestion and the family quarrel are potent spurs to philosophy – not least in suggesting a few good New Year resolutions to follow.

Poverty's Price

According to the song inspired by Ezekiel, one of the Old Testament's more colourful prophets, 'The ankle-bone is connected to the shin-bone,' a skeletal platitude intended as an illustration of the truth that all things are linked. Two events occurred in the week in which these words were written, between them painfully exemplifying this ancient truth despite being separated by a pair of oceans, one of water and the other of silence.

One was a meeting in Cancun, Mexico, of the World Trade Organisation. The other was a London arms fair at which the latest lines in tanks, missiles and fighter planes were on sale. Eyes tend to glaze at the mention of agricultural subsidies, which was the topic of the Cancun meeting; and shoulders tend to shrug fatalistically at the mention of arms sales, especially when the billions of dollars and thousands of jobs at stake in Western economies spring to mind.

But no one has to be an earnest moralist to be troubled by the juxtaposition at issue. At the best of times matters of justice and humanity have a feeble grip on the attention of comfortably busy people – as the majority in the Western world are – but sheer self-interest should be enough to make them pay attention. This is because the connection between farming and arming threatens disaster for us all.

The aim of the Cancun meeting was to discuss the negative effect on developing countries of the agricultural subsidies paid in rich countries. This is not simply a matter of the strange arithmetic of world economics, in which each European cow is subsidised to the tune of $2.50 per day while two billion humans elsewhere in the world each lives on half that sum per day. Rather, it is that the subsidised rich-world overproduction of foodstuffs results in dumping on Third World markets, under-cutting the prices of the latter's own products. For example: superfluous European sugar is sold in Africa at prices well below the production cost of the sugar which is Mozambique's main crop.

It does not take rocket science to understand the con-sequences. But rocket science is busy elsewhere: a single cruise missile costs a million dollars, an aircraft carrier one and a half billion dollars, a new Kalashnikov automatic rifle $500 – though a second-hand Kalashnikov (the world is awash with them) costs one small child in an East African bazaar. (Children are currency in poor regions where local civil wars are the chief event.) The world spends more than $30 billion every year on arms – which is to say: on the means of killing people and destroying the homes and workplaces of survivors. One British-made cluster bomb costs the same as thirty annual incomes in rural Africa. Think what these sums could do in places where people walk miles each day to fetch clean water, and where schools and clinics, if they exist at all, are rudimentary beyond belief. While resources are so massively misdirected, and while injustices in their distribution are so openly perpetuated by their bene-ficiaries, the only certainty is future trouble.

Poverty threatens world stability in many ways. Although people struggling at subsistence levels are generally too hungry, exhausted and ignorant to rise up against a dispensation that negates their human potential – what a pang it gives to think how many village Hampdens and mute inglorious Miltons exhibit their ribcages to the African dust – there comes a time when resentment begins to grow. And then comes trouble: first as local internecine conflicts, making matters even worse, and then as terrorism fuelled by the resources of the desperate, including religious fundamentalism as the place in which angry young men find the simulacra of pride and hope – leading to racism, xenophobia and hatred of the rich world whose unjust practices keep the poor world down.

The answer has never lain solely with 'aid' from rich to poor nations, some of which anyway just goes to fund yet more arms purchases by the latter, fuelling problems instead of funding solutions. Rather, it is to allow the Third World to earn its own living, which it would do if the rich world's trade barriers and subsidies were reduced. Rich-world politicians fear their powerful rural lobbies, and when a French farmer says, 'Why cannot French taxpayers pay me to preserve our traditional French agriculture and landscape?' one can see why. But the long-term consequence of stoking anger in the poor world is that there will eventually be not just no French farming left, but no French taxpayers, and indeed no rich world – for untended poverty eventually eats up riches everywhere.

Knowledge

When Karl the Great, King of the Lombards and Franks, better known as Charlemagne by the nation which claims him for its own, set about instituting general elementary education in his domains, he wrote a capitulary stating the principle that motivated him. 'Right action is better than knowledge,' he wrote, 'but in order to do what is right, we must know what is right.' Some say that when the quest for knowledge is carried too far it paralyses action; but this mistakes a crucial point, which is that there is something greater than either knowledge or action, and that is understanding, which grows from the conjuncture of both; and which prompts the need for more of both in its turn.

Charlemagne's far-sighted educational endeavours resulted, in succeeding generations, in increasing numbers of men (women of course were excluded) acquiring a thirst to know more and to discuss what they had learned. They congregated in Paris, like moths to a flame, from all quarters of northern Europe. Thus was born the first *studium generale* north of the Alps: the University of Paris. Its students were eager to hear about the best that had been thought and said about logic, rhetoric, arithmetic, geometry, astronomy, theology and music. That was the curriculum of the day, preparing students for further study towards the three great professions of law, medicine and the Church.

To modern eyes Paris University's founding curriculum has a quaint look about it. But in the conditions of the time its aim was worthy, for it sought to address the human mind's many sides by training, broadening and equipping it, thereby preparing it for the effective action Charlemagne cared about.

In essentials, that is what a university still is: a place where the extension of knowledge and the equipping of intellect go together, to make it possible that all sorts of action can be right. It also of course serves the enrichment of the individual: Aristotle said, 'We educate ourselves so that we can make noble use of our leisure.' But that is an adjunct of Charlemagne's goal; for the considered life, the well-lived life and the effective life go mutually together as the same thing.

Universities have had a roller-coaster history in Britain, seen from a bird's-eye view. Oxford was a scion of Paris, and Cambridge of Oxford, and in their early centuries served the same purpose in the same way. But in the Renaissance the new humanistic learning took place outside the universities, which soon became stuck in the stagnating mire of their old curricula, and eventually began to drown, as Gibbon acidly put it, in their prejudices and port. They became ineffectual finishing schools for boys who had learned more Latin and Greek at their schools than the ancient universities could teach them.

The reforms of the nineteenth century rescued them, under pressure from the example of the new civic universities, modelled on cutting-edge dissenting academies which had led the way by teaching modern languages and sciences while Oxbridge's dons dozed among their decanters. For a hundred years the ideal of rounded, independent and intellectually lively universities, combining teaching and research, aiming at excellence and taking the best minds among school-leavers to expand and furnish them, was the unquestioned norm.

By the close of the twentieth century talk of universities, at least in Britain, was talk of a different and scarcely recognisable kind of institution. For two or three decades beforehand British universities were treated as soft targets for financial cuts and neglect, and were then disastrously hit by a series of follies: first the mere renaming of polytechnics as universities, then by doubling student numbers without commensurate funding, and finally, in an effort to slow the resulting collapse of standards and facilities, by various bureaucratic devices of coercion aimed at 'measuring' teaching and research quality, thus further diminishing both while being supposed to maintain them.

Of the crowded, peeling, straining, labouring institutions called universities in early twenty-first-century Britain only two could be regarded by objective measures as having international standing. Certain others had departments which merited the same description, but the country as a whole had slipped drastically from its position as a centre of world-class higher education. One does not need a university degree to consider what this meant in economic and social comparisons, although so badly placed were most British universities that employers were beginning to think that a university degree was no longer worth much, preferring to train their staff themselves.

Kant said that life's three great questions are: What can I do? What ought I do? What can I hope for? Applying them to universities, one sees that governments seek only to answer the first, and then only in terms of what re-electable budgeting minimalistically allows.

Empire

When the Prime Minister of Sri Lanka visited Washington, the White House issued a press statement saying: 'The President will welcome the Prime Minister of Sri Lanka to the White House. The President and the Prime Minister will review the status of the peace process in Sri Lanka.' What does that sound like? A visit of equals? Of course not. Unmistakably, it was the visit of a satrap to his emperor, a client-ruler bending his knee before the source of power, seeking approval.

Nothing could better illustrate the position of the United States in the early twenty-first century world. It has long been a cliché to describe it as an imperial power, the Rome of our times (with Europe, so Europeans hopefully murmur, as its Athens). The comparison with imperial Rome is older than Gore Vidal's satirical application of it, or than the debate over whether it is correct to describe the American version of power without ownership – and it seems, curiously, without responsibility – as 'empire' in the strict sense. But the US's solitary eminence in military and financial might makes the comparison all the more interesting – and, arguably, not wholly apt.

It is interesting because America's client-states, whom it calls 'allies' for purposes of encouragement or propaganda as need dictates, are very like satrapies in the ancient sense. The term 'satrap' originated with the Medes, whose term *kishatrapavan* meant 'a protector of a province'. Their organisational methods were adopted by the Persian empire which followed, and especially by its two greatest Great Kings, Cyrus and Darius, who divided their immense domains into twenty satrapies and set their tribute. The satraps became in effect little kings. They in their own turn appointed governors over districts, and as long as the military units in each satrapy remained under the Great King's direct control, the system worked well. Alexander the Great adopted the model, and so in their turn did the Romans, although at first Roman provincial governors gave themselves fewer airs than Persian satraps did.

In the heyday of the Persian arrangements it was common to see a satrap, invincible among his own, present himself at the capital city of Persepolis to kneel at the imperial throne for a blessing or rebuke. Or the emperor might process through his dominions, receiving the obeisance of the satraps at each provincial capital. When Sri Lanka's Prime Minister visits Washington, or the US President visits London, both events have much of these imperial courtesies about them. And the entourage of assistants, dignitaries, advisers and guards which, in full panoply, accompany the imperial progress, was then as now a visible sign of the principal imperial commodity: power.

Other comparisons might be drawn too; but if they are to hold fully between the United States and these ancient models it will have to be late Rome which is invoked, for it illustrates what happens when a great empire's frontiers – the places where its power is stretched to the fullest limit – begin to look vulnerable. The Roman example is striking, for the frontiers in question are uncannily the very regions where the military aspect of American policy was being tested as the twenty-first century ceased being new.

Until its handsome Indian summer under the Antonines in the second century AD, the Roman Empire was never overpressed by difficulties, simultaneous or not, along its vast borders, which ranged from Hadrian's Wall in the furthest north to the natural frontier of the Rhine and Danube, and on to the client tribes of Arabs who patrolled the sands beyond Syria and Judaea on its behalf. Plenty of difficulties occurred, and simultaneously; and Rome found it wise not to try conquering too much (the Germans taught them that). But until Marcus Aurelius's useless son Commodus became emperor in AD 180, the frontiers, though troubled, were held.

But then men and money began to run short, and Rome faltered. The eastern provinces of Armenia, Assyria and Mesopotamia had to be abandoned to the Sassanians, and unceasing hostilities threatened all the European borders. The western and eastern halves of the Empire tore apart, the former succumbing to waves of Gothic invasion, the latter increasingly turning its face east, from whence – in fact, from what is now Iraq, and the sandy deserts south of the Euphrates – its greatest challenges, and eventual overthrow, came.

But here is a difference. Whereas it took Rome five centuries to learn about limits, America, unquestioned world hegemon only since 1989 when the Soviet Empire unravelled and the Berlin Wall fell, was, by the new century, already doing so.

Europe

When Pieter Bruegel painted a significant event, such as Icarus plunging into the sea or Christ staggering under his cross on the slopes of Calvary, it is invariably tucked away, scarcely noticeable, in the tumult and distraction of surrounding daily life. The Icarus painting, for example, seems to be about a farmer hunched over his plough in the foreground; as one's gaze wanders across the canvas it picks up, as if by accident, a distant splash in the sea far beyond the ploughman's straining back – and that is Icarus going with melted wings to his death.

Many big events of history are like the meaning of a Bruegel painting, their central significance obscured in the heat and dust raised by irrelevancies. Such was the enlargement of the European Union from fifteen to twenty-five members in the spring of 2004. For some – those whose past dreams and present insecurities made them anxious about Europe's advancing inclusiveness – it offered merely an exacerbation of problems about immigration and security. Their anxieties might have been objectively understandable, but in truth they were based on a lack of a sense of history in two directions, neither grasping what the best future offered, nor understanding the larger past.

A century or more in the future, united Europeans might look back at the first century of their great adventure with wry condescension for the divisive, petty and unimaginative hesitancies of those who wished to suck their thumbs in the illusory comfort of a status quo which, had they succeeded, would have crumbled around them, pitching their left-behind corner of the continent into second-world status. These nay-sayers are nationalists or the like, who strangely think that the fissured Europe which produced the twentieth century's two world wars, in which tens of millions died, is a Europe that must be preserved for ever.

Their narrow vision is explained by their ignorance of Europe's larger and longer history. Fissured Europe, the Europe of nationalistic wars and the still-failing experiment of the 'nation-state', seeded and nurtured from the jealous shadows of racism and xenophobia, is a recent Europe, no older than the nineteenth century in concrete fact, though those seeds were planted at the Treaty of Westphalia in 1648. That treaty ended the hideous century of wars of religion following the Reformation, which began on 31 October 1517 when Luther nailed his ninety-five theses to the church door of Wittenberg, objecting to certain money-raising practices of the Church.

Before then, and for a hundred years afterwards, Europe was a single arena, parcelled out in shifting arrangements among the members of a widely extended royal family multiply inter-related by blood and marriage, and highly regionalised under a feudal or quasi-feudal system. Dialects and even languages differed markedly within a few miles of one another, so that there was no sense of someone's being (say) German rather than Saxon, Bavarian or Prussian.

England became a single country only a thousand years ago, when King Edmund of Wessex claimed overlordship of the kingdoms of Mercia, York and Northumberland in AD 944, and his son Eadwig invented the title King of England in 954. Even then unification was incomplete; Lothian, a part of the old kingdom of Northumbria, remained an independent Saxon statelet until it was invaded and annexed by the Scots in 973. A domestic British empire in which England dominated all of geographical Britain and Ireland was not complete until the beginning of the nineteenth century, predating the unification of Italy and Germany by a few decades only.

Just a few centuries ago Sweden and Lithuania had great

European empires. Forced unions existed under Napoleon and Hitler, the difference between them being that the former was a good thing (Napoleon emancipated the Jews, demolished the vestiges of feudalism and introduced a noble system of laws), whereas the latter was in every respect the negative of the former.

Europe's internal borders have never ceased shifting. They did so again when the European Union enlarged to twenty-five members. A decade before that, the Czech lands of Bohemia and Moravia separated from Slovakia, and Yugoslavia split into three or (depending on how you count) five countries. In the past, including the recent Balkan past, borders were changed by war: every historical boundary in Europe, in fact, is drawn in human blood. The peaceful fission of Czechs and Slovaks was a rarity. Their rejoining under the EU umbrella happened peacefully, peace (and prosperity) being the splendid gift of the EU adventure.

Were Bruegel painting an allegory of today's EU expansion, in the noisy foreground would be a quarrelling crowd, while others in the quiet background shake hands. This latter, Bruegel would mean, is the main event.

Fences

In building a fence around their country to keep out suicide bombers and other enemies, the Israelis followed copious historical precedent. In ancient China, starting as early perhaps as the seventh century BC, stretches of wall were raised by various states as a defence against neighbours. Tradition says that in the third century BC the First Emperor of unified China, Qin Shi, linked them to make the first true Great Wall. His wall was repaired and extended in the Ming dynasty (fourteenth to seventeenth centuries AD), eventually reaching a length of 1,500 miles from the shores of the Liaodeng Gulf in the east to the fortress of Jiayuguan in the Gobi Desert, far to the west. Its purpose was to keep out northern barbarians – among them the Mongols and later the Tartars.

I have seen both ends of China's Great Wall. There is a great resemblance between the landscape around Jiayuguan and the shimmering beige vista one sees from the north end of the Dead Sea, at Shuneh, looking across to Jericho. At night the Gobi Desert is lit by a fiercely burning medley of stars; from Shuneh on the Dead Sea one sees the lights of Jerusalem strung like tangled pearls on the close horizon. Jiayuguan is testimony to the hopeless ambition represented by walls and barriers everywhere, throughout history. From Shuneh one sees the unhappy, tormented, disputed, tragic land where yet another barrier stands newly raised, as if nearly three thousand years of failed experiments with the idea counted for nothing.

The philosophy of the fence had established itself independently in all parts of the world long before Qin Shi Huang

Di joined up the pieces of the Chinese wall. For many centuries afterwards no self-respecting city lacked its walls and towers, no manor house its moat and palisade. In AD 132 the Emperor Hadrian built a wall across the neck of Great Britain to keep out the lice-ridden Pictish thieves who, incapable of civilisation on their own account, existed by plundering the rich Roman province to their south. A century later the Emperor Septimius Severus rebuilt the wall more securely; it had a ditch in front of a rampart, with a road behind, and with forts, towers and blockhouses regularly intermitting its length.

Most of these structures were devised to keep unwanted people out, whether from a house, a city or a country – or even, as in Northern Ireland, from one part of a suburb. Building walls to keep people in was a refinement that reached its height with the Jewish ghettos first of Venice and then of other European cities. It was a simple application of the means used by herdsmen to corral their animals, and had about the same degree of tenderness. In the barren decades of Soviet hegemony over eastern Europe, the Iron Curtain took the literal form of electric fences and a Berlin Wall to the same end.

Two thoughts must forcibly strike anyone who contemplates this historical plethora of walls and fences. One is that none of them in the end ever succeeded, anywhere, in keeping anyone out, or in. They were useless, a uselessness so repeatedly and resoundingly proved by events that it is astonishing to find a government in our own day spending millions on erecting another. The futility of the gesture is a measure of the desperation, and the tragedy, prompting it – a desperation felt, and a tragedy suffered, on both sides of the fence planted in that troubled and bloody ground west of the Dead Sea.

The second thought is that physical fences only rise when mental fences have already been built. And it is of course the mental fences that are the real problem. Hatred and hostility, arising from fear or from insults and injuries real or perceived, and feeding under the disguises of racism, religious intolerance and territorial jealousy, inevitably result in the erection of barriers between people and peoples. Once separated, they come together only to fight. The barriers make matters progressively worse, because as distance and ignorance increase it becomes harder for opponents to work their way back to mutual understanding, to reach compromises, and in the process to make painful but essential concessions.

When individuals get to know one another it is usually impossible for them to like or hate each other on the basis merely of generalities about race, religion or history. To hate successfully, you must hate an abstraction – the totality of Arabs or Jews or whomever – because once you put a face to a person, and with it a home, children, an enjoyment of hamburgers or football, all abstractions melt.

Obviously – so obviously – to prevent the atrocities that abstract enmities prompt, the requirement is for hatreds to be dismantled, not fences erected.

Information

There is instructive irony in the fact that when members of Brick Lane's Bangladeshi community complained about Monica Ali's eponymous Booker shortlisted novel, the United Nations was meeting in Geneva to discuss censorship. Officially the topic of the UN meeting was the internet and communications, but it was about more than what is euphemistically called 'internet governance' because it also had the worthy aim of promoting the supply of all forms of communication technology to every community in the world.

But it is precisely this ambition of global access to information that some, in the same spirit as Monica Ali's Brick Lane critics, oppose; for they feel threatened by views different from their own, and therefore wish to censor them. That is what the phrase 'internet governance' masks, for in the aspiration of countries such as China and groups such as Christian and Islamic fundamentalists, it means not just protection against spam, hate speech and obscenity, but silencing of anything opposed to their own point of view.

Censorship is an ancient evil, and liberation from it is the fuel of progress. The word derives from the Censors who conducted ancient Rome's five-yearly census and watched over its public morals. Famously, Cato the Censor once expelled a citizen from the Senate because he had kissed his wife in public. But this was not censorship in the modern sense. In classical Athens earlier, censorship – at least of the enfranchised parts of the population – was anathema; and its freedom of thought and expression was the very stuff of the intellectual flowering that gave birth to the West.

When Johann Gutenberg introduced printing to Europe in 1450, censorship as we now know it came into its own. So many books flew from the new presses that within decades the Church found it necessary to act against their 'erroneous and pernicious' effect. An unofficial index of prohibited books had existed since literacy became more general in medieval times, but an official Index was instituted in 1559, and in its lifetime (it was abolished in 1966) every major work of science, literature and philosophy appeared on it.

The opposite of censorship is freedom of expression. A distinction exists between freedom of opinion and freedom of expression, in the sense that even under the Inquisition or the Taliban one could think what one liked, as long as one did not say it. But the freedom to express views, verbally or in writing, is a late, incomplete and localised right in human history, chiefly a post-Enlightenment privilege of members of Western nations. Even so it remains circumscribed in various ways, either by custom or law, mainly in the interests of social order and cohesion. But governments even of avowedly liberal stamp, such as those in Europe and America, can suffer the general tendency of all polities towards restrictions on civil rights, for example when liberty-curtailing anti-terrorist measures are introduced; and freedom of speech can be compromised along with them in the name of security. When that happens, a victory has been conceded to those who would deprive the free of their liberties altogether.

Freedom of expression means little unless it is conjoined with access to information. As Jesuits and mullahs know ('Give me the boy until he is seven and I will give you the man,' is a Jesuit motto), closing a mind by schooling it thoroughly and early into a particular world-view, and thereafter limiting access to alternative views and inconvenient facts, is an excellent way to impose automatic and permanent censorship over that mind. But human intelligence has a way of opening itself to new ideas, which is why the second component of the censorious strategy – limiting access to information – is so important to ideologues. The internet's cornucopia of competing ideas, opinions, information, attitudes, propaganda, inducements, seductions and suggestions is no threat to a mind already open; but to the closed mind hitherto tied to a set outlook it can be revolutionary. This is just what that strange assortment of bedfellows which includes China's Communist Party, America's Baptists, and traditionalist mullahs, do not like. At the UN they tried to do to the internet what Monica Ali's critics wished to do to her novel; and they will doubtless keep on trying.

The first champion of free speech is John Milton. His powerful essay against censorship, the 'Areopagitica', resulted within decades in abandonment of censorship laws in England, and a century later in the US's constitutional right to freedom of expression. The modern world owes an enormous debt to both events, and therefore to Milton's inspiration of them. Whenever the UN meets to discuss internet access, and in places like Brick Lane, Milton's arguments still apply.

Mr Dean and Job

It seems that Mr Howard Dean, when he was temporarily front-runner for nomination as Democratic Party presidential candidate in the United States in the year 2004, had to furbish his religious credentials preparatory to visiting his country's Bible Belt – the southern states, home to the Southern Baptists and many other 'bible-believing' and 'born-again' sects. Noticing that he had so far failed to mention the deity in any of his election speeches, he decided to remedy matters by volunteering the information that he knew the Bible well. When asked which New Testament book was his favourite. He replied, 'The Book of Job.'

There would have been no greater risk to Mr Dean's chances of becoming President if he had said '*Oliver Twist*'. Americans do not require their presidential candidates to display much factual knowledge; the incumbent President, Mr George W. Bush, enjoyed a well-known pre-election blank concerning world geography (and much else), as evidenced in interviews, a fact greeted with equanimity by a sufficient plurality of voters to get him the White House job. In the same spirit, Mr Dean's advisers doubtless calculated that approving mention of the Bible is enough to charm Bible Belt ears, whether or not he was genuinely acquainted with its contents.

But Mr Dean's citing of Job was puzzling. Of all scriptures it gives least comfort to apologists for the God of the Old Testament (where, in case you share Mr Dean's level of acquaintance with the Bible, it belongs). This God is in origin a volcano deity – manifesting itself in fire and burning bushes atop mountains, and in pillars of smoke – and he is an arbitrary tyrant of egre-giously murderous habits. Regretting that he created humans, he drowned them all except for Noah's family, presumably hoping to restart history; but with no happy result, for he had to continue frequently striking people dead, from Onan (of the misdirected seed) to the thousands who disagreed with Moses about the proper management of Israel's wanderings, and whom he therefore swallowed en masse in a great hole. And so, numer-ously, on.

The story of Job caps all. To win a bet with Satan over Job's faith, God kills Job's seven sons and three daughters, and des-troys his wealth and health. When Job justifiably complains of this treatment, God bullies him, the tenor of his argument being that since he is far mightier than Job – 'Where wast thou', he asked, 'when I laid the foundations of the earth?' – he can do what he likes: might is right. It is not for Job to question God's actions, including the infliction of wholly undeserved tortures.

We are supposed to take comfort from the fact that God in the end restores Job's wealth and gives him more children. (According to some scholars this is a later addition, when the need for an upbeat ending was recognised by priests anxious that their flock might seek elsewhere for milder and more just deities – who were, after all, the ancient world's insurance companies; for though rarely reliable they were all that was available). No parent in our own more godless age would regard God's belated remedy as compensation for lost children – pre-sumably large quantities of faith are needed to think otherwise.

The Job story is intended to illustrate the virtue of absolute obedience and blind faith. But this is not the aspect of religion uppermost in Bible Belt observance. Contemporary Christianity cherry-picks its Bible teachings, ignoring injunctions to give all your money to the poor, to repudiate your family, to give no thought to the morrow, etc., for Christianity is an unliveable creed for all but desert anchorites. Rather, the significance of 'Bible-believing' in the southern states is akin to that of Roman public religion in classical times. As a mixture of social bond and national good-luck charm, worship at the temples of Jupiter, Mars and other approved deities was a public duty in ancient Rome, and anyone who refused it was regarded as that most subversive of creatures, an atheist. Atheism was punishable by death. The Romans regarded the Christians as atheists because they rejected the state's tutelary gods, and therefore punished them accordingly. Hence Nero's attack on them in AD 64, the first of Rome's ultimately futile attempts to extirpate this new version of the ancient but ever-recurrent Oriental legend of a hero or god who visits the underworld and returns, a legend which repeated itself often before its Christian version, from Osiris in Egypt to Orpheus with his lyre among the Maenads.

As in Rome, where public office was closed to anyone who did not profess the public gods, so in the Bible Belt. It is the profession of faith, not its content, that seems to matter; which is why if Mr Dean had claimed that Genesis is an alternative name for the Apocalypse, he would not thereby have injured his chances one jot.

Schism

After the assembled primates of the Anglican Communion had discussed the problem posed by the ordination of an openly gay American bishop, they issued a statement containing a striking phrase. They said that the ordination threatened to 'tear the fabric of our communion at its deepest level'. From an ancient Greek word, *skizein*, originally meaning 'to rip, tear or cut cloth' comes the word to which the Anglican primates thus delicately allude: 'schism'.

As a technical term of theology and canon law, 'schism' means an organisational rupture in an ecclesiastical unity, turning one church into two or more. From the earliest times a distinction was drawn between heresy and schism, the former defined as perversion of dogma, the latter as separation from the Church. But as St Jerome recognised, heresy-involving differences over dogma are the chief reason for most schisms anyway. 'By false doctrine heretics wound the faith,' said St Augustine, 'by iniquitous dissensions schismatics deviate from fraternal charity.'

Well might these early Church Fathers ponder such matters, for their religion is a ferociously schismatic one. As early as AD 63, just thirty years after the death of its founding figure, the Jewish Christians of Jerusalem split from the gentile church then being built by St Paul. The unedifying tale is told in the Acts of the Apostles; a sticking point, so to say, was the vital question of circumcision. While that was happening St Paul was writing to the chronically argumentative and fissiparous Corinthians, 'I beseech you, brethren ... let there be no schisms among you,' for the process threatening the Anglican communion, which in recent times gave us the fragmentation of the Church of Scotland into a Free Church, a Wee Free Church and a Wee Wee Free Church (like a set of acrimonious Russian dolls taking each other to court over church property and funds), had already begun.

So many were the schisms of the early Latin Church that no century passed without at least two major cases. Typical in their causes were, for example, the schisms of Hippolytus in AD 217 and of Novatian in AD 251, namely, their conviction that their respective Popes did not punish sinners and apostates harshly enough. Doctrinal quarrels involving Arians, Gnostics, Nestorians, Pelagians and many more – each of these labelled 'heresies' by the side that won the argument – resulted in schisms and persecutions, the latter intended to nullify the former.

But the two greatest schisms in Christendom proved unamenable to punitive solutions. The first is the Great Schism of the East, in which the Latin Church of western Europe parted from the Orthodox communions in the east. The separation of the Roman Empire's western and eastern halves, and the increasing importance of Constantinople thereafter, was the starting point, although the process was a long and gradual one. It was only formally accepted after the failure of the Council of Florence in 1439, despite having been *de facto* the case for seven centuries. Greek, Russian, Serbian and other Orthodox communions looked to the Ecumenical Patriarchs of Constantinople as their *primi inter pares*, but the Patriarchs never had the authority of Rome's Popes, who for their part thought that the whole Church, east and west, owed obedience to them as St Peter's linear successors.

The second Great Schism is usually regarded as the circumstance of the Latin Church having two Popes, one in Avignon. But in reality it was the Reformation. The Protestant churches that came into existence after Luther's nailing of theses to the Wittenberg church door in 1517 have never ceased to proliferate. Multiplying like bacteria by constant fission, there are now over 20,000 separate Churches in the United States alone. Accordingly the Reformation should perhaps be renamed the Great Ongoing Schisms. In accordance with the truth that 'divided they fall', for most of the period since the Reformation the west's churches have been diminishing forces. Even where evangelical versions have lately flourished, as in America and West Africa, it is on the seductive basis of treating material prosperity in this life as a divine reward, in defiance of scriptural teaching to the contrary.

The threatened schism within Anglicanism turned on a scriptural teaching which some Anglicans are not minded to defy, namely, the proscription of homosexuality in Leviticus 18: 22. Here schism seems to be the right answer, for a church which does not accept gay people fully seems well worth schisming from.

Holy Sites and Unholy Rows

There is only one novelty – but it is a tragic one – about long-running and dangerous disputes such as those over the Temple Mount in Jerusalem and the site of the Babri mosque in Ayodhya, India, and that is that when they take a violent turn, Kalashnikovs and Semtex have superseded more traditional clubs and daggers as the language of the fray. In all other respects the profound inter-religious animosities excited by these 'holy sites' – animosities scarcely flattering to the deities allegedly associated with them – are nothing new in the history of human folly.

When the Mughal ruler Aurangzeb demolished Hindu temples and forced conversions to Islam at the point of the sword in late seventeenth-century India, or when the Crusaders invaded medieval Palestine to 'recover' Biblical sites for Christendom by force, they were reprising well-established historical patterns. An examination of the religious complexities of ancient Greece, for example, shows that the Olympic pantheon, and the myths explaining the relationships among its members, record the imposition of one set of cults upon another. Thus Zeus, a sky god brought into Greece by northern invaders, conquered the earth gods and especially their queen, Hera. By the time assimilation had done its work, Hera was Zeus's wife, and the sky-dwelling gods dined regularly with those who lived on and under the ground, at a suitable meeting point halfway between: a mountain peak.

Expert opinion does not now much endorse *Golden Bough* Frazer's theories, but there is innate plausibility in his account of how Catholic veneration of the Virgin Mary has its roots in the great cult of Diana, virgin goddess, whose shrine at Ariccia on the shores of Lake Nemi was the Roman world's most sacred and popular centre of pilgrimage – it was Lourdes, Delphi, Jerusalem and Ayodhya rolled into one. To seduce worshippers from Diana to Christianity, the Church in its post-Constantine flush of first power took the simple course of informing her votaries that a great secret could at last be revealed to them: that her real name was Mary.

To the secular view, squabbles over supposed 'holy places' constitute yet another dispiriting, not to say contemptible, chapter in the long and disgraceful story of superstition, stupidity and collective madness too characteristic of religion and the crushing burdens it imposes on mankind. To votaries of the warring faiths, the anguish of having their holiest symbols and places polluted and blasphemed by unbelievers is immense – a psychological assault so great, indeed, that they are prepared to kill and die to defend them.

The difference between these viewpoints is stark. The secularist longs to liberate mankind from the superstitions that divide and murder. The faithful long to enjoy the treasures of their faith secure from the depredations of others – and, too often, to erase the infamy of the others' false gods and evil observances, especially if they claim to occupy the very ground on which their own sacred past has its habitation.

Of course the solutions are as simple as they are impracticable. One is to stop brainwashing children into the superstitions of their ancestors, so that they can grow up thinking for themselves. Rather few people would find any religion credible if first offered it for consideration when they are rational adults. (The lonely, the insecure, the frail of heart might always succumb to the easy, comfortable promises of religion in its contemporary disguises; they would not find its more traditional blood-and-thunder forms as tempting; think of, say, seventeenth-century Calvinism.)

An equally obvious and simple solution, and a more likely though still tenuous one, is for different faith groups to learn to live together and share sacred sites. Proof that this can be done lies in the fact that it has been done: *'ab esse ad posse'*, as the philosophers say. Jerusalem is itself a case in point. But of course the risk remains that when other factors – politics, events elsewhere in the world – go wrong, the place tensions are most felt is where there is too great contiguity. The Temple Mount and the site of the Babri mosque are the ultimates in contiguity: the very same pieces of ground, the very soil under the surface, are each the selfsame thing belonging to two different traditions whose claims to them (unlike the thousands of other places in the world where one religion has succeeded another yet adopted the same site) are still acutely alive.

The parenthesis in this last point is important. In the infancy of human understanding, when religion was mankind's first science and technology – science because it offered explanations of natural phenomena, technology because it offered a means, by prayer and sacrifice, to influence them – certain places came to be deemed sacred, either for their special character or because particularly significant events occurred there. Sacredness implies what is set apart for the use of supernatural agencies and their intercourse with mankind; they acquire importance as the dread locations where communicating with the gods, or drawing down their power, or averting their wrath, seems possible. It is natural therefore that a site sacred in one religion should be taken over by a superseding religion brought by, say, conquerors. It would scarcely be surprising if a dark and dreamy grove on a mountain served as holy to peoples widely separated in historical terms, simply because it has that goose-pimple feel of a place where the murmur of wind-stirred leaves sounds to the credulous, nervous or admiring sensibility like the whispering of angels.

The only thing that can save the Temple Mount and Ayodhya from being excuses for further bloodbaths is if two bold, imaginative and magnanimous leaders arise, one on each side, who agree to put the tortured past behind them. The solutions cannot be particular to the disputed sites; their hope lies in general settlements of the wider tensions. While these persist, the sites themselves are merely running sores on which problems, like flies, accumulate. Putting bandages on them will not cure the larger disease – the sad and perennial disease of religion-inspired hatreds among men. For that, a new world is required.

Resurrection

From the ubiquity of resurrection myths in the world's religions, it is obvious that the life-and-death question of the vegetation cycle provided one of mankind's earliest impulses to superstition. Myths relating to the winter death of plants and their revival in spring probably became organised when mankind first engaged in settled agriculture about 10,000 years ago, thereby giving rise to systematic religions with priesthoods and ritual.

The ancient Egyptians saw their god every day, and felt his power on their backs; for he was Ra, the sun. When he wandered southwards as each year's autumn drew into winter, his votaries became anxious that he would not return – which meant that the crops would fail and they would starve. They therefore sacrificed a human being to him on the winter solstice, and dismembered the body to scatter it like fertiliser on the fields. Characteristically for a deity, Ra liked the taste of murder, and duly returned.

But the allegory of the demise and revival of vegetation itself was embodied in another major figure of the Egyptian pantheon: Osiris. His brother Seth killed him, and his sister (and wife) Isis brought him back to life. He too was chopped into pieces and scattered across the fields by Seth, all but one interesting piece of him being found and reassembled by Isis. This intertwining of love and death is a persistent theme in the myths; in the case of Persephone, daughter of the corn goddess Demeter, it is Hades' passion for her which makes him kidnap her into his underworld kingdom – whence, after her mother's intercession, she is allowed to revisit the upper world for two thirds of the year – from spring to autumn, naturally.

Mesopotamia's Dumuzi (in the Bible, Tammuz) was for 4,000 years mourned annually when he went for his exile in the underworld, and greeted with rejoicing when he returned. Canaan's Baal had to descend annually into the underworld to fight Mot, King of Death, and the forces of disorder; an early legend has him murdered by his brother and brought back to life by his sister (and wife) Anat. In Hittite religion, Telepinu allegorises the annual death and resurrection of nature; he goes missing, and when found is stung back to life by a bee (suggesting an early guess at plant embryology).

Far from these Middle Eastern myths – which sometimes evolved into non-religious tales too, as of Orpheus, Odysseus and Heracles, all of whom made return visits to the underworld – the same themes persist. Mali's Pemba had to die and regrow as a tree in order to create human souls from the bark. Odin of the Norsemen hanged himself from the World Tree, Yggdrasil, in order to drink from the fountain of knowledge in Hell. Nana-huatl of the Aztecs cremated himself so that he could rise again as the sun. Tayau of the Huichol Indians, son of their corn goddess, was thrown into an oven, and travelled underground to emerge in the east also as the sun. And so on and on. The list is long.

In the context of these many tales the Christian 'story of Easter' is a mythopoeic cliché. As with Orpheus, Odin and Odysseus, the descent into and return from Hades is detached from immediate connection with agriculture, but it offers a kind of salvation not much different from escape from starvation, for in the theology of St Paul the prize is escape from death. For Odin and Odysseus, by contrast, the prize was knowledge, while for Orpheus it was love. Knowledge and love are far nobler prizes than mere prolongation of existence, and it is doubtful whether eternal prolongation of existence is anyway desirable just as such (especially if it involves endless hymn-singing).

The Aztecs have it that their gods cremated themselves to give birth to mankind. Now there is a heartening allegory! If only all the gods in whose name people currently kill one another would cremate themselves and thus liberate mankind from the bane of religion, how much happier a place the world would be.

Enquiry

It has been well said that one should not be so open-minded that one's brains fall out. This is a good admonition to those who, for example, pusillanimously declare themselves agnostics when the only rational alternative to belief in the existence of supernatural beings can be atheism. This is because the basis of belief in the existence of gods and goddesses is no different from that for belief in pixies, namely legend and credulity; and the grounds for entertaining the thought that something might exist (footprints, fur snagged on fences, grunting in the night, actually seeing the creature in question bounding upon a hillside), require much better and more consistent supports than the pre-scientific fictions invented by our ancestors to explain what they did not understand.

People forget how strong the belief in the Little People was until quite recently – they were a feature of things well into Victorian times, and even later. They were blamed for much, such as missing pins and curdled milk, the lights seen on the marshes, and various aches and twinges suffered by old ladies. As reason diffused its happy light over the Western hemisphere, courtesy of the growth of literacy in those same times, belief in pixies and their ilk faded.

But superstition has strong talons; a lady of Cork, literate and generally sensible, was once asked whether she believed in leprechauns, and replied, 'I do not; but they are there anyway,' thus beautifully capturing the spirit of agnosticism in all its faint-hearted fence-sitting tendentiousness; for it is premised on the fact that since no one has proved that X does *not* exist,

X might exist, as if this in any way followed, and as if responsible and disciplined intellectual endeavour does not show the fallacy of thinking that, for example, the fact that no one has proved the non-existence of Tolkein's Hobbits means that they therefore might exist in some Middle Earth after all.

Still: it remains important to be open-minded, though with a disciplined readiness to subject what is offered for our intellectual assent to stringent evaluation by the light of probability and experience. These two latter are indispensable servants of thought. They explain the difference between the assiduity with which some seek the Loch Ness Monster, while no such expense of cameras and microphones, boats and planes, bearded researchers and photojournalists has ever clustered around the possibility that a woodland grove might be the scene of moonlit pixy parties. For the idea of large marine beasts has a plausibility endowed by whales and manatees, while the idea of antique such beasts has its plausibility from sharks and coelacanths, both of them survivors from hideous depths of zoological time.

Oddly, it is the credulous who are least open-minded. They accept dogma, and dogma closes – even indeed punishes – enquiry thereafter. Voltaire says that he honours the man who seeks truth, but despises the man who claims to have found it. That saying touches the essence of the difference exceedingly well, and should be the motto of anyone who aspires to intellectual honesty.

Democracy

Democracy substitutes election by the incompetent many for appointment by the corrupt few.

GEORGE BERNARD SHAW

Democracy can deliver some nasty surprises. Yet 'democracy' is a feel-good word; it is what the West officially stands for. Who in normal circumstances would dream of saying – at least, aloud – that oligarchy, plutocracy or dictatorship is preferable? The standard cliché is: democracy is bad, but the alternatives are worse.

Democracy has not always been so cherished. In fact Western civilisation has been anti-democratic for most of its history, with democracy until recently vilified as the despotism of poor, ignorant, unthinking majorities over better-off and better-educated minorities. Since most of those able to record their opinions belonged to the latter class, history is filled with their condemnation of the concept.

In its 'democratic' phases classical Athens was not a democracy. Women, slaves and aliens had no say, and men only reached adulthood at the age of thirty. But at its height under Pericles, Athens' version of democracy produced art, architecture, drama and philosophy of such power and excellence that they still shape Western civilisation.

Yet even then democracy had opponents. The aristocratic Plato attacked it for putting management of the state into the hands of ignoramuses unable to distinguish right from wrong. He blamed it for making the citizenry 'idle, cowardly, loquacious and greedy' and for devouring those – Pericles, Miltiades, Themistocles – who had given it to them in the first place.

With Athens' philosophers against it, democracy had little chance among later thinkers. Renaissance writers were convinced that it meant limitless tumult. Enlightenment moralists saw it as a threat to virtue. America's founding fathers believed it led to a dangerous equalisation of property. And when the grudging shift to quasi-democracy happened in Britain in the century to 1930, its opponents claimed they were being sold to the rabble. For them, democracy meant the terrifying Paris ochlocracy of the early 1790s.

What has lately made democracy not just respectable but something to die for? One answer is: the work of nineteenth-century historians, who rescued Athenian democracy from the opprobrium of earlier historians. This is a plausible thesis, for intellectual sentiment diffuses itself like dew in the night, and democratic ideas are not the only ones to achieve resurrection because later thinkers reversed their predecessors' judgements. By associating its ideals with the glories of Periclean Athens, revisionary historians made democracy respectable.

But democracy is only truly respectable if its method of delivery is good. It requires a system of representation which yields stable government without being numb to the smaller legitimate interests that abound in modern societies. This means a middle path between the British system, which disenfranchises many and permanently results in minority-based governments, and the weak, fragile, temporary coalitions of recent Italy, or the Israeli model, where tiny fringe parties (chiefly of ultra-religious zealots) hold the balance.

But above all democracy needs a thoughtful electorate who actually vote – compulsorily, if necessary. 'Voter apathy' is blamed on politicians; it is in fact the fault of ignorant, lazy, indifferent or complacent non-voters themselves.

As simplifications go, the following contain some truth.

Right-wingers are in politics to protect their own interests, left-wingers are in politics out of concern for others. The former are amenable to almost any compromises that subserve their ends, the latter are passionate and ultra-democratic to the extent, often, of making themselves unelectable because of splits and feuds.

Democracy's capacity to shock has been its own demise: witness Chile and Algeria – and indifference harms it too: witness the first election of President George W. Bush. When time next brings in its revenges, what kind of -ocracy or -archy will result? And how will those who abuse or neglect their democratic responsibilities enjoy being even less in control of affairs than they now are?

Debate

The aim of debate should not be victory, but progress.

JOSEPH JOUBERT

One duty of responsible journalism is supposed to be reasoned discussion of public affairs. Tabloid newspapers in most countries have a notorious tendency to avoid that duty, providing their readers instead with a more profitable diet of scandals, secrets, outrages, surprises, conflicts, splits, quarrels, sex, celebrities, television-related gossip, and sport – standardly in a mixture of several at once.

It is an all too familiar fact that the stridency and superficiality of tabloid contributions to public debate wreck our politics. When members of a government or political party internally discuss ideas, trying to explore different points of view and approaches in formulating policy, their efforts are invariably represented as evidence of splits and enmities, as if having a debate were a weakness. The resulting atmosphere makes it more difficult for governments to find rational means to well-chosen ends.

But the most serious product of the tabloid mentality is its undermining of thought about crucial social questions, the kind on which public opinion needs to be fully and responsibly informed. Liberalising legislation on prostitution, pornography and obscenity, keeping religion out of the public domain, abandoning blasphemy laws, and legalising some or all drugs, are among the central questions on which most politicians and policemen are afraid to express a view, for fear of the salacious, sanctimonious, nasty war that would be declared upon them by the tabloid mentality. Our resulting inability to have a sensible public debate about such things is a principal reason why we suffer chronically from the problems they cause.

The key lies in the fact that the tabloid attitude is not concerned with the public interest, but only with what it thinks interests the public. Tabloids are partisans not of the truth or the good of society, but of the profits shown on next quarter's balance sheet. Conflict and scandal sell newspapers, so if neither arises by itself, the tabloids will seek them out or make them up. Of course no one begrudges honestly made profit. But tabloid profits are not always honestly made. They are too often made out of the stuff of the sewers, and smell the worse for it.

'The partisan engaged in a debate cares nothing about what is right,' Socrates says in one of Plato's dialogues, 'but only to persuade others to agree with him.' True debaters are not, therefore, partisan. They share a concern to arrive at truth, or sound judgement, or the best result, or an increase of understanding. When they criticise and disagree, it is the opposing argument and not the opposing arguer they address, for they know the reverse technique is a cheap fallacy of logic. And wherever they find an opposing argument strong, they rejoice to have learned something thereby.

Rhetoric

Much of the really important business done at party-political conferences and conventions is doubtless transacted behind the scenes, in hotel bars and private rooms. For the rest of the population, in so far as it pays attention, party conferences are about big set speeches and how they are received. They matter, because a standing ovation and good reviews in the papers can keep a politician secure for another few weeks or months – a long time in that perilous trade.

In this sense speeches matter. If they are effective it is because they succeed in being essays in the art of rhetoric, wrought to achieve a predetermined effect; written with skill and care if possible, but at least with acute awareness of possible unintended interpretations and pitfalls, for which they are combed by advisers; and they are rehearsed beforehand.

Such preparation does not guarantee eloquence, but eloquence is not the point. Eloquence is an innate gift, rhetoric is a child of art. An uneducated person can be supremely eloquent when moved by sorrow, indignation, or an earnest desire to publish the truth. The rhetorician is in a quite different case. The less he is governed by feeling, the more effective he is. The contrast lies in the degree of consciousness involved. Eloquence is typically unselfconscious, springing from natural emotion and a sincere desire to communicate what the speaker feels and thinks. Rhetoric is deliberate and (in the literal sense of this term) artificial; it carefully weighs its audience, deploying tropes and techniques specifically designed to achieve its end, which in every case is to get that audience to agree with the speaker, or anyway to support him. Rhetoric is wholly about persuasion.

Of course eloquence persuades too, and sometimes more powerfully than rhetoric. But eloquence can have other aims. It can inform, amuse, entertain, enlighten, encourage, inspire. These too might be used by the rhetorician as subordinate to the goal of persuasion. But equally they can be, and often are, self-standing aims, requiring nothing from the audience beyond what it is willing to give.

That is not enough for the rhetorician. He is single-mindedly determined to get the audience onside. Rhetoric was first formulated as a science and taught for a fee in classical antiquity, when a man's career, and sometimes his life, depended on his ability to sway audiences. The teachers of this science were called Sophists, and they claimed they could 'make the worse case appear the better', and move an audience to agree both with a proposition and its negation. For this reason Socrates despised them. He held truth to be paramount, so if rhetoric disguised it, or led hearers to falsehood, then it was wicked. He believed in what he called 'dialectic' rather than rhetoric, meaning by it a co-operative search for truth by means of enquiry and questioning. In dialectic, matter matters more than manner, whereas in rhetoric, manner is almost all.

And this is why rhetoric gets a bad name. Its techniques include anything that will work: appeals to the audience's emotions and self-interest, wit, creativity with facts, anecdotes, attacks on opponents whether relevant or not, even 'body language'. The old chestnut about the man who murdered his parents and then asked for clemency because he was an orphan, illustrates even as it caricatures rhetoric's essence.

There is usually nothing so crude in political speeches. But that only means more care is required of those listening to them, in separating rhetorical manner from the matter it conveys – or cloaks.

Conversation

Everything that happens in the human realm, leaving aside external accidents such as disease and earthquake, comes down to some individual deciding 'yes' or 'no' about another individual. This is a sobering fact. It is also a useful one to know, since it means that the chief instrument of advancement in life is simple and obvious. It is: getting the right person on your side at the right time.

Add to this the familiar fact that the deepest satisfactions in life come from personal relationships – loves and friendships – and we see that in the end everything good in life ultimately depends on how adept we are at conversation.

If this seems too large a claim, remember that conversation, properly understood, is the whole vehicle of personal interaction. There are of course important non-verbal forms of interaction, largely reserved to occasions when clothing is an inconvenience; and social psychologists are quick to remind us that non-verbal utterance is as important as words – body posture, gesture, and the like.

But these are part of conversation too, for the term embraces all human communication. By talking of the 'conversation of mankind' some even include literature and art as contributions to humanity's discussion with itself. This notion is a good one, because the opposite of conversation in all its senses is silence – not the silence of peace, but of stasis, ignorance, and night.

There is a distinction between more and less formal conversation, ranging from the courtroom to the bus queue. The places where paradigmatic conversation occurs are of course social occasions. Plutarch used this fact to make an instructive point in his 'Moral Essays' about the well-lived life. Describing the Dinner of the Seven Sages, he has one of them observe that although everyone knows what preparations a host must make, few reflect on those required of guests. Sybarites liked to have their dinner invitations a year in advance in order to think about what to wear, but this, said Plutarch, is not what he had in mind. Rather, a guest's preparation must be education and courtesy, so that he can participate well in conversation. And that means knowing not just how to speak well but, even more importantly, how to listen attentively and question intelligently. Eight centuries later he was echoed in La Rochefoucauld's maxim that 'to listen closely and reply well is conversation's highest perfection'.

The other great conversational virtue is discretion. The argumentative boor is as much a pain as the endless bore and the monosyllabic boar. Discretion recognises the life-saving qualities of the vague generality, as George Ade pointed out, and at the same time knows that too much agreement stifles conversation, as Eldridge Cleaver observed. Discretion means knowing when to speak, what not to say, when to stop, and how to deflect a conversation when a doubtful turn has been taken. To be a good conversationalist, in short, is to be a friend to mankind, and the reward is to be befriended by mankind in return.

Why War?

In 1932, on the hundredth anniversary of the publication of Carl von Clausewitz's *On War*, Albert Einstein wrote to Sigmund Freud to ask, 'Why war?' He had come to see that science cannot explain the fact that human beings, uniquely among animals, kill their own kind in highly organised ways, channelling vast resources into doing so. In common with Bertrand Russell he felt that the only defence against future war is world government. What, he asked, did Freud think?

Einstein had been invited by the League of Nations to examine the problem of war by writing publicly to a correspondent of his choice. He chose Freud in the hope that the new theory of psychoanalysis might offer a diagnosis and, with luck, a cure. Freud's answer – it is one of history's more delicate ironies that he dedicated it to Mussolini – was pessimistic. Violence and inequality, he replied, are natural to mankind. Historical evolution sees weak people banding together to oppose strong individuals, their collective strength eventually constituting a legal order. Such an order might one day bring about 'the eagerly desired reign of "everlasting" peace', but only by the 'paradoxical' means of the collective's power to wage war on warmongers. But a utopian state of peace, Freud admitted, is only 'theoretically conceivable', because in practice inequality, aggression and strife are endemic to human existence.

In this answer there is neither real diagnosis nor real cure. It assumes the naturalness of man's violence towards man, and sees collective aggression as the sum of individual aggression. But neither assumption is convincingly explored. Other animals are aggressive, but in specific and self-limiting ways: males compete for mates, females protect their young, all are wont to squabble over food. But fights invariably end when one combatant flees or submits. Apart from man, animals do not prey on their own kind. A troop of baboons might drive away territorial invaders, but will not pursue them to enslave or kill them. Similarly, social animals often seek new territory in search of food, but they do not seek to enlarge existing territory by conquest. Man alone does such things.

Whatever explains war, therefore, has to be sought elsewhere, in the complexity of man's economic, political and psychological constitution. And here suggestions are legion.

On one view, wars are attempts to solve political and economic problems during periods of international instability. Wars involve massive redirection of productive and social forces, thereby easing – if only temporarily – the pressures that cause them. Moreover they quicken the pace of technological innovation, and by setting massive logistical problems for governments they sometimes creatively forge new political and administrative possibilities.

Marxist analysis is somewhat similar. It sees war as a tool by which national monopoly capitalisms struggle to gain advantage over each other. On both the historical and Marxist views, states do not stumble accidentally into war, but choose it as a deliberate means of securing influence and control of productive resources.

These analyses say that war is about power, wealth, control. They say that wars are instruments in the hands of political and commercial interests; they are what leaders get us into. Fortunately for such leaders, these analysts point out, demagoguery on the simplistic themes of nationalism and patriotism can be counted on to rouse enough young men for slaughter to follow.

The twentieth century's major wars might not exactly fit these theories, but their joint effect was indeed to shift power and redirect wealth: they weakened Europe and established the United States as supreme in the economic and military spheres. The only other combatants to benefit in the longer term were those who were so heavily defeated that they could restructure from scratch, unhampered by illusions of past glory and the burdens of victory. And like many wars, they were revolutionary in impact: Lenin's Soviet Union was created by the First World War, Mao's China by the Second.

One of the less optimistic observations on which analysts of all stripes agree is that war is no longer so containable a process. Vast leaps in military technology have made it total and potentially final. And as Adorno said, the power of modern weaponry shows that we are cleverer, but not wiser, than our ancestors, for we have merely substituted the intercontinental ballistic missile for the spear, but we still behave like cavemen, motivated by greed and fear and unable to resist fights.

It is instructive to listen to views about war expressed before technology reached its horror-story proportions. There are sane voices – those for example of Sun Tzu, the ancient Chinese theoretician of war, who argued that it is better to achieve one's aims by negotiation than by 'bloodied swords', and Richard Cobden, Victorian free-trader, who indefatigably opposed war on the grounds that it harms commerce and hinders progress.

Cobden was, alas, one of the nineteenth century's few unequivocal adversaries of war. Much exemplary nonsense was written on the subject by his contemporaries, extolling war's benefits in promoting virility, purifying the race, and enhancing creativity. Clausewitz argued that war gives nations their place in the world, while simultaneously purging their peoples of 'effeminacy and degeneracy'. Proudhon regarded war as integral to human identity. Engels was eerily correct in his anticipations of modern warfare, predicting terrible slaughter and the despoilation of Europe. Like Cobden but unlike Clausewitz he regarded war as ungovernable once started, and unstoppable until it exhausts itself; but he nevertheless thought it has a place in the dialectic of history, as the way capitalism will destroy itself.

It is dismaying to find Thomas de Quincey and John Ruskin among romanticisers of war. The opium-eater describes war as a 'physical necessity' for man, arguing that it 'purifies and redeems itself' by bringing greater evils than itself to an end. In this latter respect de Quincey is right; the war against Nazism was necessary in just this way. But the 'evils' he had in mind were not of that sort; he meant, for example, England slipping behind in the international race for raw materials and markets.

Both de Quincey and Ruskin decried the mechanisation of war, which meant the passing of courtly conflict, the end of chivalrous jousts between knights under fluttering banners. They saw no romance in artillery and mud. Ruskin especially had an aesthetic view of war; once, he wrote, it was a sublime enterprise, in which 'Every man put on a crown, when the band of flute-players gave the signal for attack; all the shields of the line glittered with their high polish, and mingled their splendour with the dark red of the purple mantles.' Men were sanctified by combat, from which rose all that is highest in culture. 'There is no great art possible to a nation,' said Ruskin, 'but that which is based on battle.'

Such nonsense is, however, harmless in comparison to eugenic theories. Darwinism led some to treat war as a mechanism of natural selection. General Sir Reginald Hart applauded war's 'extermination of inferior individuals and nations'. Heinrich von Treitschke argued that war is compassionate because it rescues the weak and feeble from their misery. His view did not go unchallenged: G. F. Nicolai argued that war is actually dysgenic, because the fittest and best march off to be slaughtered, leaving the unfit at home to father children.

But the only certainty of war is the one implicit in the Delphic oracle's answer to Croesus, when he enquired whether he should wage war on Persia. 'If you do,' said the oracle, 'you will destroy a great empire.' Heartened, Croesus went to war, and did indeed destroy a great empire: his own.

The oracle's answer reminds us that there are always losers in war. Sometimes the greatest losers are the victors. It might be necessary to defend one's freedoms, or to combat such evils as Nazism; so there are justifiable wars, and we have to be prepared to fight them. But in its inception and character there is a profound madness in war. To organise murder on the large scale – to plan it, to conduct scientific research into it, to build its instruments in factories, to train men for it, to applaud them when they do it; or, on the passive side of the equation, to sit silent when bombed houses, spread-eagled bodies, weeping refugees, waste and destruction appear on our television screens – suggests that we have embraced as normal something vastly ugly and diseased. Perhaps Einstein's question should not have been, 'Why war?' but 'How can we possibly tolerate its existence?'

Just War

To anyone of humane and pacific instincts, the phrase 'a just war' looks like a contradiction. But a moment's thought shows otherwise. The idea that war, however ugly in itself, is sometimes unqualifiedly just is amply demonstrated by the example of the Second World War, a struggle which provides the focal case of a legitimate use of violence to defend against aggression and to put an end to oppression and genocide.

The theory of just war stems from St Thomas Aquinas. In Part Two of his *Summa Theologiae* he examined the proposition 'that it is always sinful to wage war', and argued to the contrary that, on three conditions, war can be just. The conditions are, first, that there is a just cause of war, secondly, that it is begun on proper authority, and thirdly, that it is waged with the right intention, meaning that it aims at 'the advancement of good, or the avoidance of evil'.

To these conditions modern theorists have added two others: that to be just a war must have a reasonable chance of success, and that the means used to conduct it must be proportional to the ends sought. The first addition is a pragmatic one; one gloss is that a leadership commits an injustice against its own people if it leads them into a war they are sure to lose. A problem with transforming this prudential consideration into a moral one is that it seems, by contrast, rather immoral, not to say spineless, to avoid engaging in an otherwise just war because it threatens to be too costly. When the Polish cavalry galloped towards Hitler's Panzers in defence of their homeland, they were going futilely to war, but their courage gave them a moral victory, and was an inspiration to others.

The second addition is a controversial one, for as war leaders otherwise as different in outlook as Churchill and Mao Zedong both emphatically held, once involved in a war there is no mileage in fighting with one hand tied behind one's back. As Mao succinctly put it, 'War is not crochet.' Whether this justifies using nuclear weapons or poison gas is a very moot point. This involves questions not of what makes it just to go to war, but of what counts as acting justly once engaged in war – the difference between the *justum bellum* and the *jus in bello*. As the Second World War shows, a war might be a *justum bellum* and yet lack *jus in bello*, as the British bombing of Dresden and the American attacks on Hiroshima and Nagasaki arguably illustrate.

Aquinas's original three conditions are, however, clear and persuasive in themselves, offering what is from the point of view of ethics the unusual gift of an unambiguous set of principles. Difficulty enters when a case has to be made for whether the circumstances of a given case are such that the principles of just war apply, especially as regards the first and third, for they respectively always prompt the questions: does such-and-such really count as a just cause for going to war? and: are the aims for the intended war good ones?

There are clear examples of a just cause for going to war. Defence against aggression is one, as is going to the rescue of people being subjected to aggression. Is it equally just to engage in pre-emptive military action against a potential aggressor? The lesson of history teaches that appeasement and inaction are dangerous tactics; but how can one be sure that an unfulfilled threat is genuinely dangerous, and can one be sure that alleging a threat is not a mask for one's own aggression? On the other hand, a people has a right to defend itself, and the best form of defence is to prevent attack in the first place – by diplomacy if possible, but by force if necessary. A leadership fails its people if it does not prevent them from being harmed by aggressors.

What might count as just war aims? Aquinas said: promoting the good or avoiding evil. By this is meant that a war waged for such reasons as self-interest, *Lebensraum*, other people's oil fields, or pure aggrandisement, is not justified. 'Avoiding evil' can be invoked by those seeking to defend themselves preventatively, and – if they are right about the threat posed by a delinquent regime amassing dangerous weapons – with justification. The positive aim, that of promoting good, which must at least involve bringing about peace, stability, democracy, prosperity, and a situation in which both victor and defeated can cease to be enemies, is equally easy to identify. Too many wars, whether just in their inception or not, fail to achieve this outcome, because the harder struggle of 'winning the peace' is too often fudged or dodged.

Although the Aquinas conditions are clear and compelling, they can never, just by themselves, count as sufficient conditions for going to war. Other considerations apply. Have all diplomatic means failed? Is there consensus over the 'just cause' and 'right intentions' requirements among all parties implicated on the side of the intending belligerent? Are there no means other than military action to bring about the desired aims? In practice, diplomacy and various forms of pressure, including sanctions, are the standard means for adjusting international disagreements (and those within a state that threaten civil war), and in most cases actual military conflict is a last resort, whether just or not. Certainly it seems hard to describe a war as just if it is not a last resort, after sterling efforts have been to find other routes away from conflict.

The truly just war would be the war of ideas which ended by rooting out the greed, stupidity, superstition and ignorance which lie at the ultimate roots of all human conflicts. Only in that utopian dispensation will it be possible to beat swords into ploughshares and shell casings into scales of justice. Until then people will fight; sometimes, with justice, for freedom and life.

Tyrants

It is instructive to note that there is a natural link, one that perhaps recognises the existence of an inevitable progression, between the two standard definitions of the word 'tyrant'. One tells us that a tyrant is an absolute ruler – that is, one who governs without restraint or limitation. The second tells us that a tyrant is one who rules oppressively and cruelly. Acton famously remarked that all power corrupts, but absolute power corrupts absolutely, and history bears him out. 'Oh that the Roman people had only one neck!' complained Caligula, a sentiment that all his tribe, from Nero to Hitler, Stalin and Pol Pot, would recognise and – thinking of their enemies – applaud.

The downfall of tyrannies and tyrants prompts such rejoicing that it is a mystery how they ever come to exist. If people are so keen on liberty, and so hate its enemies, how is it that most forms of rule throughout history have been tyrannies or the next best thing? Part of the answer lies in a telling comment made by Steve Biko six years before his death in a Pretoria police cell: 'The most potent weapon in the hands of the oppressor', he said, 'is the mind of the oppressed.' Once in the thrall of oppression, individuals willy-nilly become its agents: they censor and police themselves, their fear makes them betrayers of others, they see their only self-defence in surrender, they carry out tyranny's murderous dictates in order to protect themselves and their families. It takes superlative courage to resist the impulse in each individual to escape harm. The resisters of tyranny are mankind's greatest heroes.

But the foregoing explains only the continuance of tyranny.

Its beginning is an even sadder matter; for it is in the laziness and inattention of majorities that tyranny finds its toehold, so that by the time people bethink themselves, it is too late to bestir themselves. Maybe they even welcome it at first: how many people believe that the answer to problems of a social, political and economic kind is a 'strong leader', a guide – a Führer. They only fully realise their error when the Führer's leather-coated police knock on their front doors in the early hours.

From the tyrant's point of view once he (or she: remember Ci Xi of China, and she was not alone) has begun on a course of oppression – of 'disappearing' opponents, filling mass graves, torturing and raping, starting wars, and so forth – it is impossible to stop. He rides a tiger and dare not dismount. A tragic inevitability enters the picture: the only plausible limit to a tyrant's career is death, often enough precipitated by revolution, as in Ceauşescu's case, or assassination, as in the case of Caligula and Nero. Whoever heard of a tyrant voluntarily laying down his power, unless it be to a chosen successor, an heir, intended to have as absolute a sway?

By the same token, whoever heard of a tyrant promoting gentle laws, liberties, welfare, love, enlightenment? Most tyrants know enough to provide bread and circuses to keep the mob distracted, if not content; or to keep them hard at it, at war perhaps or anyway hating others – foreigners – and blaming them for the problems at home, thus stirring a sense of siege. Mostly, though, fear is the instrument of control, and for that a theatre of fear is essential. A lesson taught by the events of the heady epoch of 1989 is that tyrants are cardboard figures merely, when stripped of the guns and secret policemen who convey the brute impression of their power. It is regrettable but unsurprising that although everyone knows there are not enough soldiers and policemen in any tyranny to kill all the citizens if they rose as one, such things infrequently happen. But they did in 1989, and the figures of supposed power in one after another

Eastern European country showed themselves to be thin, impotent weaklings behind the mock-up of uniforms, medals, and dark glasses, high up on their balconies. Alas, the one place where the citizen protest did not prevail was where the movements of 1989 began: in Tiananmen Square, at the gates of the Forbidden City.

Each of the latest tyrants to fall has, apparently, invoked the earliest of tyranny's excuses for what it does: necessity ('necessity, the tyrant's plea, excused his devilish deeds'). In one way this is right: staying on the tiger's back makes for many hard necessities – to be borne by others, not the tyrant himself. That is why, when he falls, the only mourners are those who stood to gain by being his henchmen and executioners.

Might

Do not expect justice where might is right.

History is dogged by the tragic fact that, whenever individuals or countries become powerful they apply the crude and ancient principle that might is right, and concomitantly refuse to subordinate their power to wider and higher law. Yet it is precisely the adoption of the rule of law that has marked each faltering step towards civilising the human condition.

In a work of perceptive genius, Aeschylus was the first to celebrate the start of this process; in his *Eumenides*, third in his great dramatic trilogy *The Oresteia*, he tells of how the old rule of revenge and blood feud was replaced by a due process of law before a civil jury. Orestes, pursued by the Furies for killing his mother in revenge for her murder of his father Agamemnon, throws himself on the mercy of the goddess Athene. She convenes a court with a jury of Athenian citizens – the first ever – to try his case, which maddens the Furies, who accuse her and the other 'young gods' of usurping the rights of the 'old gods' whom they represent. Athene placates them by giving them an honourable home in her city of Athens, and thereafter the concept of a due process of law replaces might as the arbiter of right – at least, among the good and wise. This is one reason why classical Greece is the crucible of Western civilisation.

Aeschylus's drama told in symbolic form of the crucial moment in Athenian history when the warrior virtues of courage, endurance and military preparedness – an ethos that persisted in the tough arrangements of Sparta long afterwards – were replaced by the civic virtues required for life in community. The achievement was the work of the great law-givers Solon and Pericles, who saw that a community could never flourish as long as inequities persisted between the powerful few and the oppressed many. When Solon gave his laws to Athens he said that their intention was to offer justice to all, expressly so that the less strong would not be preyed upon. He then travelled abroad for ten years, having secured the Athenians' agreement not to alter his laws for that period, so giving them time to work. (It was while he was travelling that he met the fabulously wealthy King Croesus, who asked him to say who was the happiest man on earth, expecting himself to be nominated – only to get the disconcerting reply, 'Call no man happy until he is dead.')

Athens' law-givers were putting to work an obvious enough truth. As Thomas Aldrich much later put it, 'The possession of unlimited power will make a despot of almost any man. There is a possible Nero in the gentlest creature that walks.' This pessimistic but not inaccurate view explains much, from the excesses of absolute rulers like Caligula and Nero, to the behaviour of pocket tyrants like the 'kapos' in Nazi concentration camps. 'To be a great autocrat you must be a great barbarian,' said Joseph Conrad; but the thought applies generally. The only restraint on the tendency of power to debase its holders, and to take the shortest way to getting its ends – summary executions, torture, war, the use of terror and repression – is a structure of law, with proper methods and independent judges, before whom even a ruler must be answerable.

Two and a half thousand years after the leap taken by classical Athens towards the civilising government of justice, the administration of President George W. Bush showed itself neither good nor wise in repudiating the efforts of the rest of the world to make all mankind a domain of law – for that is what the United

Nations' International Criminal Court (which President Bush's predecessor, Bill Clinton, supported) is aimed at doing. Bush's reversal of Clinton's policy suggested that the mentality of the lone Wild West gunslinger persists in conservative American exceptionalism – except when, as persistently and inescapably happens, the United States finds itself in need of allies abroad.

Heroism

My hero is he who wins praise without bloodshed.

MARTIAL

The active participants in most contemporary conflicts are doubtless thought heroes by the constituencies of anger they represent. They include the suicide bomber, the *jihadi* with his Kalashnikov in a mountain cave, the sectarian with his club and firebrand intent on murder. In all cases they oppose well-equipped professional soldiers, who in their turn are thought heroic by those who see them as protectors of order or (say) democratic values. Heroism is typically thought a warrior virtue, and it is true that, in the absence of enough fanaticism or rage to make it unnecessary, it indeed takes courage to fight implacable enemies with guns and bombs, given that they answer in kind.

In self-defence against malign aggression, or in the interests of principle, such courage would deserve the name of heroism. But all other fighting and killing, squabbling and destroying, never do. On the contrary, heroism is first and foremost the property of peacemakers. It takes infinitely greater courage to salvage a people or an epoch from conflict than to start or continue it. The outstanding figures of our time, among whom Nelson Mandela is the exemplar, are those who seek reconciliation, agreement, forgiveness – very milksop notions, no doubt, in the view of people who think it cleverer to let their guns do their thinking and talking. Such folk would scarcely merit even our contempt if it were not that their way of solving problems does such fantastic harm, and if it were not that there is a massive organised means of supplying the wherewithal for it, namely the arms trade. Those who oppose them not with returned gunfire but with offers of peace are as high above them morally as Everest is above a worm cast.

Nathaniel Hawthorne remarked that 'a hero cannot be a hero unless in an heroic world'. This is profoundly untrue. It is when the world has become sullied and degraded by violent quarrels, when reason has yielded to frenzy, when all human feeling has been boiled into hatred, that true heroism might flourish if it can be found. Part of the reason is that the first thing peacemakers usually have to face is the animosity of their own side, which regards them as traitors and weaklings. They will be in the uncomfortable position, at least for a time, of being better regarded by enemies than friends. The people who could best thank them, if they were able to understand what was done for them, would be those not yet born – next year's children, or in the longer term the beneficiaries of a generation which had the blessing of growing up in peace.

The medieval Muslim sage Sa'di wrote, 'Even if you could tear the head off an elephant, if you are without humanity you are no hero.' That is the key. There is a quiet but not-so-small heroism of the moral life which is crucial here. It is very much easier to be intolerant, angry, jealous and resentful than it is to be generous, patient, kind and considerate. Without question it takes far more thought, and far more work, to treat others from the standpoint of these virtues than from that of those vices, which is why the latter are so prevalent.

Each of the world's current conflicts needs just two individuals, leaders on opposing sides, to stand up, meet, talk, keep clearly in view some image – a child blinded or limbless because of bombing, say – and to agree a fixed determination not to use large-scale murder as a way of managing differences. On that basis real hope can enter the picture. This is of course an extremely hard thing to achieve; but it is why such individuals, if they were to appear, would be heroes indeed.

Sacrifice

In the pre-classical age of Greece, when the Homeric epics still existed in oral form only, the idea not just of sacrifice but of great sacrifice was a very familiar one. Agamemnon's act of killing his daughter Iphigenia to placate an angry goddess doubtless chilled the blood because of the nature of the tie between sacrificer and victim, but the largeness of the act would have been no surprise, especially given the purpose in hand, which was to allow the tremendous expedition against Troy to go ahead. Think what a tiny place the Greek world was in the Mycenaean age, and therefore what an investment of time, wealth and manpower went into building and equipping that immense military expedition of a thousand ships. To be delayed by the anger of a goddess was a disaster in the circumstances, and the sacrifice required to remove the obstacle of her anger, in the light of the sacrifices already made, needed to be commensurate. And so it was.

The Greek idea of great sacrifice came to be proverbial. Many centuries after the classical age, when the American thinker Emerson visited the English poet Landor in Italy, it was to hear the latter make a wonderful remark: 'Every man', said Landor, 'must slaughter his hundred oxen, whether or not he knows they will be eaten by gods or flies.' This is a reference to the ancient Greek practice of the hecatomb, the sacrifice of a hundred oxen all at once, as an especially significant offering to the gods. A hundred oxen represented a large part of the community's wealth, so it was a sign of serious intent: the community sought to impress the gods by the earnestness thus displayed, and they were prepared to give up much to get the point across.

Among the Greeks of the Archaic and Classical periods, sacrifice was in essence a form of worship, and it was based on the ancient and universal anthropomorphic belief that the gods have much the same needs as men – a roof over their heads, a table on which to eat (the altar), food and clothing. One of the standard sacrifices to the goddess Athene was a dress called a *peplos*. Drink was given to the gods in the form of a libation, which meant pouring out wine, milk or blood onto the altar or the ground. Animals were killed on the altar, and one third of their meat was burned there as an offering, another third going to the priest (of course), and the remaining third to the donor of the animal. On special occasions the entire animal was sacrificed to the gods, all of it being burned on the altar; this was known as a *holocaust*, and it was the kind of sacrifice made when some special evil had to be dispelled.

One form of sacrifice among the Greeks involved destroying or otherwise parting from something valued or cherished, as a way of proving modesty before the gods and avoiding their jealousy. This was because displaying a degree of happiness or wealth too great for the normal human condition was to risk inviting the angry attentions of the goddess Nemesis, whose job was to punish such pretension. The most famous example of a mortal attempting to avoid the gods' jealousy occurs in the story of Polycrates, a very successful businessman and shipowner who seized power in his native island of Samos and turned it into a great market and trading port, with an attached leisure centre very popular with sailors from all round the Mediterranean. He and Samos became fabulously rich, and he surrounded himself with artists, philosophers and writers, among them the lyric poet Anacreon. Naturally apprehensive that the gods might think he was rivalling them in splendour, he threw his most expensive ring into the sea in the hope that they would not deprive him of the rest of his wealth. Alas, to no avail. In those unsettled times there were always wars to be fought; in one of them Polycrates was lured into an ambush by the Satrap of Magnesia, and was killed – as it happens, by being crucified.

The idea of sacrifice can have, and has often had, disagreeable applications. The strange genius of the philosopher Nietzsche gives an example. In stating his doctrine of the 'Superman' – the powerful, positive, life-affirming individual who overcomes the trammels of conventional morality in order to live heroically and supremely – Nietzsche allowed himself to contemplate the following idea: 'Mankind sacrificed en masse so that one single stronger species of man might thrive – that would be progress.' The idea was appropriated by Nazism, even though Nietzsche was strongly opposed to anti-Semitism and German nationalism – and one can well see why. It is at the least an ambiguous application of the idea of sacrifice, even though elsewhere in his writings Nietzsche rather whimsically hopes that the majority of mankind, recognising its own feebleness and inability to 'overcome' itself as required by a Superman, will sacrifice itself on the altar of the future.

The practice of influencing or soothing the supernatural powers that govern the affairs of men by giving something up, or by killing, breaking or destroying something to put it beyond human use, dates from the earliest phases of the human story, as shown by its presence in all cultures in all regions of the world. But in the usual way of social evolution, sacrifice has had markedly different forms and come to serve many different subordinate aims over time. In the nineteenth century, when anthropology first became an organised discipline – impelled by the colonial experiences of the European powers and their encounter with a wide variety of traditional cultures – one of the phenomena that immediately demanded attention was sacrifice. Peruvians, Aztecs, Polynesian islanders and West African tribes between them sacrificially killed thousands of people every year until colonisers outlawed the practice. Missionaries viewed as demonic the ritual killing of animals followed by washing in or drinking the victims' blood, and tried to stamp it out likewise.

But even as colonists and missionaries intervened in the old rituals, so anthropologists were trying to understand them, not least because they recognised the connection to their own allegedly civilised religious culture, in which the body and blood of a sacrificial victim is consumed on a weekly basis – happily, in symbolic form – and in which sanguinary tales, such as that of a father preparing to slit his son's throat in obedience to God's command, fill the holy literature of the tradition. For they saw in this variety of sacrificial practices the application of beliefs about atonement, purification and supplication.

The earliest systematic anthropological theories had it that sacrifice originated as the offering of gifts to the spirits, in the hope of securing their favour or minimising their hostility. More detailed studies gave rise to more elaborate views, not least the famous theory put forward by William Robertson Smith in his influential book *The Religion of the Semites*, in which he identified three different kinds of sacrifice: the honorific, the piacular and the mystical.

The first kind – honorific sacrifice – involved a sharing of the sacrifice between the gods and their worshippers, after the fashion of a kinship group eating together to cement the blood-bond between them. In honorific sacrifice, the gods share a meal with the worshippers as an affirmation of the bond or covenant between them.

The second kind – so-called 'piacular' sacrifice, which means the cleansing away of sin, especially of the really bad sins of sacrilege or taboo-breaking – probably started as a means of expunging the guilt of bloodshed within a kinship group; and it also probably involved the killing of the person guilty of that bloodshed in the first place. In time, a stand-in for the guilty person was found, typically the totem animal, the representative of the god. To take away the sins of the people, the god had to die – or at least his representative, a sacrificial lamb or goat.

The third – mystical – kind of sacrifice expressly involved the slaying and eating of the god himself. According to Robertson Smith, its point was that, to begin with, the gods were strangers to mankind, and in order to become kin with man they had to be incorporated within man, rather as a child is incorporated in its mother, which is its route to membership of her clan. Because animals are not kin to humans, the only way to get the god within man was to make a carefully chosen human (an 'elect of god') serve as the representative of god, and to kill and consume him in a special rite.

The Christian mass or communion service clearly mixes together all three of these kinds of sacrifice: the mystical consumption of the god, the affirming of the bond between god and man therefore, and the purging of sins by the death of the sacrificial victim.

But critics of Robertson Smith's view might be forgiven for thinking that rather than explaining the primitive origins of practices like the Christian mass, he has taken different elements of the latter and applied them in retrospective interpretation of other forms of sacrifice. It is always too easy, such critics might say, to see other or earlier forms of religion through the interpreting lens of the familiar religion of one's own culture.

Still, Robertson Smith's view is persuasive in broad outline, not just because what Christians call the Old Testament bears it out – think of Abraham and Isaac, and of the careful instructions in Leviticus about the ritual sacrifice of male animals, sprinkling their blood on the altar and making a burnt offering of the rest for the atonement of sins – but because sacrifice in almost all other religious traditions exemplifies Robertson Smith's classification too, or at the very least close cognates of it. And the way that the idea of sacrifice has spilled over from religion into moral psychology (which is to say, into our thinking about what it is truly worth doing and being in life) carries with it just these ideas of giving something up, or offering something – often, ourselves or our time, our effort, even our everything – in the interests of what we regard as a great good.

An everyday example of sacrifice in this metaphorical sense is the deferring of present pleasure for future gain. This happens when we prepare for examinations, allowing the sun to shine out of doors while we labour over our books, but with the expectation that passing the exam will bring an access of worthwhile goods or opportunities compared to which the sunshine pales. Or we refuse the offer of a slice of chocolate cake because we are dieting, making present sacrifices in the interests of future trimness. In these examples we are ourselves the beneficiaries of our sacrifices. But equally everyday are the more altruistic sacrifices people make for their children's education, or to look after an ageing parent, or to help a friend. We save money for school fees, or we give up a large part of our free time, our pleasures, the comforts of repose, to tend to the needs of someone we love who is dependent upon us.

Playing on the idea of subordinating one's own interests to those of others, patriotism asks for what it calls 'the ultimate sacrifice' – giving one's life in war. Sometimes such sacrifice is necessary, as when what is being opposed is a genuine evil, like Nazism. In such cases sacrifice is purposeful, and noble – and its nobility is not contingent upon its success; for here the main thing is that the sacrificer gave his all in the attempt itself.

More often, though, sacrifice is invited in the name of an abstraction: King and Country, the Fatherland, Freedom, something called Our Way of Life – these were what people supposed themselves to be dying for in the First World War, if they thought about it at all. Afterwards their sacrifice was rather differently viewed: not as an honourable yielding up of youthful futures in the service of a greater good, but as the useless murder of millions in a pointless war that destabilised the world and brought two generations of terribly wasteful hot and cold conflict in its wake.

The ambition of leaders in an over-armed Europe in 1914 sacrificed the future, and did little other than speed up the development of weapons technology. Talk of the 'sacrifice' of millions of individuals in this connection has a very hollow ring.

How much value a thing has for us is often a function of how much sacrifice we make to get it. A wise head once remarked that people are more likely to heed advice if they pay for it – and the reverse is true: if people get their schooling, their medical attention, and their democratic rights for free, they are apt not to put much value on them. One need only look around to see how true that unfortunately is: how many people fail to vote in elections, how much people take schools and the health service for granted. We value things properly only when we lose them; by which time it is usually too late.

The most tiresome of people are the relentlessly self-sacrificing types. George Bernard Shaw once acidly remarked that 'self-sacrifice enables us to sacrifice other people without blushing', and it is an almost universal truth that in one essential respect self-sacrificers and those who sacrifice others are alike: they both stand to gain from the sacrifice in question. Literature and the arts abound in examples of self-sacrificers – misguided self-sacrificers like Dorothea in George Eliot's *Middlemarch*, denying herself in the interests of her unpleasant dried-up stick of a husband Casaubon, or loving self-sacrificers like Liu in Puccini's *Turandot*, dying to protect Prince Calaf during Turandot's hunt for his name. Arguably, Calaf was not worthy of her. Yet on an unblinking view both Dorothea and Liu were getting more from what they gave than they lost; and if what they got was a sense of doing right, they were getting much.

There is a remarkable saying about sacrifice in the Panchatantra, a Sanskrit collection of tales ostensibly written to teach a young prince how to live wisely and to value friendship, knowledge and hard work. It goes as follows: 'For the sake of a family, an individual may be sacrificed; for the sake of a village, a family may be sacrificed; for the sake of a nation, a village may be sacrificed; for the sake of one's self, the world may be sacrificed.'

There is no part of this saying that any civilised individual could agree with, and no doubt the author of the Panchatantra, the sage Vishnusharman, did not agree with it either; but he put it into one of his tales to illustrate in summary form a common assumption, usually inexplicit, that the interest of the greater always outweighs that of the lesser, and that self-interest is the greatest interest of all. The best counterweight to this is the Enlightenment view, shared by such writers otherwise as various as David Hume, Adam Smith, Edmund Burke and William Hazlitt, that the basis of moral community is sympathy, not self-interest, and they all refused to allow the particular to be so subordinated to the general that it vanished from view. By this I mean that they saw, in true Enlightenment spirit, that the good life is an individual thing, even though it is lived in community; for the community cannot itself be good – cannot constitute the Good Society – unless each of its members is living a life he or she finds satisfying and flourishing both from the individual's own point of view and from the point of view of relationships with others. The general good is thus a function of many individual good lives; and these latter cannot be sacrificed without reducing the good of all. And arguably, if the interests, the hopes – and certainly if the life – of a single individual is sacrificed unfairly or against the individual's will, the general good is diminished thereby; not only by the loss of what is sacrificed, but by the fact that it happened at all.

I think that is what Vishnusharman meant by startling us with the assertion: 'for the sake of one's self, the whole world may be sacrificed', for the remark of course implies the very opposite of the ideas of responsibility and relationship which constitute human social bonds, and finds its expression in a celebrated remark about sacrifice with a different motive, connoting the best and truest of sacrifices, the saying: 'Greater love hath no man than this, that he lay down his life for his friends.' Too often, however, as in the case of Iphigenia, a person's life is laid down for her friends without her consent; and that is a sacrifice too far.

Crime

The great thieves lead away the little thieves.

DIOGENES

Slobodan Milosevic was the first national leader in history to be put on trial in an international court for crimes against humanity, having been indicted while still in office.

For more than half a century after the Nuremberg trials, the development of an international jurisdiction for trying national leaders was slow and faltering, opposed (as the original Universal Declaration of Human Rights was) by powerful nations who stood to be most inconvenienced by it. The US administration, for example, was reluctant to support the Hague court's trial of Milosevic, for two reasons: the expense, and the fact that America desired 'closure' on recent Balkans history so that Yugoslavia could join NATO. Realpolitik was ever the enemy of justice.

Moreover, establishing too many precedents can be unsettling for leaders of big powers. Dr Henry Kissinger, the famous or notorious right-hand man to President Nixon, had to flee Paris when he heard that a French magistrate was preparing a warrant for his arrest in connection with war crimes in Vietnam and Cambodia.

Until recently in modern times, crimes were what small people committed. When the great committed them they were called business or statesmanship. In the two centuries after Elizabeth I's time, legalised acts of criminality in the form of 'enclosures' drove the ordinary folk of England to desperation as their means of subsistence were stolen from them and they were forced into starvation, wage-slavery or vagabondage. The few gainers were those who sat (and were alone entitled to sit) in Parliament, passing the Enclosure Acts for the benefit of themselves and friends. It is one of the longest-running and baldest-faced acts of theft ever committed in the history of our green and pleasant land.

'Crime' comes from the Latin *crimen*, meaning an 'accusation' or 'reproach'. From medieval times it has been understood as an act (whether of commission of omission) forbidden by, and therefore punishable by, public law. A distinction was once made between different classes of crime – for example, between 'felony', punishment for which could include forfeiture of land and possessions as well as imprisonment or execution, and 'misdemeanour' a crime for which the most severe punishment was imprisonment.

The idea of 'crimes against humanity' is no older than 1945, and was defined as part of the juridical framework required for Nuremberg. It means an atrocity such as the extermination or enslavement of a large part of a population. 'Genocide' was coined in 1944 to denote the former large-scale crime, prompted by the Nazis' deliberate and systematic attempt to obliterate the Jews of Europe. Had Hitler won, he would have sought to extend the same courtesy to Slavs, among them, doubtlessly, the young Slobodan Milosevic.

The crimes for which rulers can now be indicted are a commonplace of history. The difference between what happened in Stalin's Russia, the Third Reich, Rwanda, Bosnia and Kosovo, Hiroshima and Nagasaki, Nanking, Dresden – this is a declension in numbers killed, not in kind of crime, which is the same in all cases, namely mass murder of civilians – and the crimes committed by Tshaka the Zulu, Genghis Khan, Crusaders in Palestine, Saracen warriors in North Africa, and so on and on, is only one of degree, made greater in the former cases by technology. If Tshaka or Genghis Khan had owned Kalashnikovs and nuclear warheads, they would have used them cheerfully. Adorno's observation accordingly bears repeating: that human progress is measured by the advance from the spear to the guided missile, showing that though humanity has grown cleverer over time, it has not grown wiser.

Except in one respect: the arrival of international tribunals founded on a determination to bring miscreant warmongering genocide-committing rulers and their regimes to account. As the Milosevic trial showed, the Hague is therefore home to one of the future's best hopes.

Juries

Imagine that you have been arrested for a crime you did not commit. You are amazed, frightened and stricken. You are locked up, perhaps for months if no bail is granted. The process of law is slow and leaden-footed. In court at last, your hope lies with a dozen of your fellow citizens, brought together at random, to hear what the prosecution and defence have to say, and to determine whether they think the prosecution makes such a strong case that the presumption everyone officially makes about you, namely that you are innocent, must be overturned.

Would you rather have your case tried by barristers and judges alone? These are people mostly drawn from a particular social and educational stratum, whose professional lives are spent considering crimes and alleged criminals brought before them by the police. Doubtless a certain jading of the palate attends the unrelieved nature of this diet. A jury of citizens, by contrast, who do not spend all their time thinking about crimes and criminals, and who are required to bring nothing but their common sense, their ordinary experience of life, and their powers of concentration, to considering whether the prosecution makes its case or not, might be expected to offer a better and fresher perspective.

More to the point still, trial by jury is a right enshrined in the Magna Carta for the protection of accused persons. A jury is the 'palladium of liberty' against arbitrary authority, for it makes the people – as represented by the jury – the judges of the law. As Lord Devlin aptly put it, 'No tyrant can afford to leave a subject's freedom in the hands of twelve of his countrymen.'

It is intensely interesting to note the special character of what a jury is supposed to do. Its task is not, despite appearances, to determine the guilt or innocence of the accused in the dock. The accused in the dock is officially presumed innocent, so what happens in a courtroom is that the prosecution attempts to persuade the jury to overturn that presumption of innocence. What the jury therefore 'tries' is the case offered by the prosecution, to see whether it is strong enough to compel them to change their minds. The defence points out flaws in the prosecution case, and directs the jurors' attention to other possibilities and explanations, so that they can thoroughly test whether the prosecution has persuaded them of the merits of its case 'beyond reasonable doubt'.

This last is a key phrase. It means that it is not enough for a jury merely to believe that the accused is guilty, but it must do so with a high degree of strength or conviction. If the jurors believe that the accused is probably guilty, but that doubts linger, and that certain possibilities cannot be ruled out – then, in conscience, they must acquit.

This loads matters against the prosecution, which has a hill to climb unless the evidence they can produce is manifestly in their favour. The police are right to say that the odds are against them in court. But they are not right to complain about it, for a determination to protect innocence is a vital safeguard in a mature and thoughtful society, even if (to iterate a point eminently worth iterating) it means sometimes letting the guilty go free.

Ultimate Punishment

By the end of the second page of Scott Turow's compelling *Ultimate Punishment* I had almost recanted my lifelong anti-capital-punishment stance. Two pages later I had regained myself. Most readers of Turow's account would probably feel the same about the cases which respectively caused such joltings of sentiment. The first concerns a man who abducted a couple at gunpoint, shot the man dead, brutally and repeatedly raped and sodomised the woman over many hours, and then killed her by strangling her and smashing her head against the floor. The loathing one feels for the perpetrator of such a crime prompts the thought that he deserves nothing better than to be exterminated as vermin.

But the second case draws one up short. It concerns a man who spent years on death row before being conclusively proved innocent. The insecurity of the man's original conviction is obvious to hindsight, the failure of his repeated appeals chilling. Caught in the machinery of an unforgiving and fatal law, he could have ended as one of the victims of a justice system which can never guarantee, even if it always worked as well as it could and ought, that it will not make mistakes. Imagine if the mistake were you.

Thus does Scott Turow, with the consummate skill of the thriller writer, portray the reasons why a society might struggle with itself over the question of capital punishment, feeling the ambivalence that Turow himself confesses at the beginning of his book. Some people are so dangerous that they have to be removed from society altogether; why should the taxpayer support them for the rest of their years? and why should their victims' families live with the knowledge that the person who permanently blighted their lives still exists somewhere, perhaps laughing at a joke, watching television, playing golf? And yet: how can we live with ourselves as a society if in cold and formal mood we kill, and in the process irreversibly risk harming the innocent? 'Better a guilty man should go free than that an innocent one should suffer,' the saying has it.

Well known for his best-selling novels, Scott Turow is also a lawyer with experience both as prosecutor and defender at the criminal bar in Chicago. Because of this he was asked by Governor George Ryan of Illinois to join a Commission of Inquiry into the use of capital punishment in that state. Ryan had himself been a pro-execution Republican before taking office in Illinois, voting for the re-establishment of capital punishment in Illinois in 1977 when he was a member of the state's legislature. But when he came to occupy the governor's mansion he was horrified to discover that over 30 per cent of those initially condemned to death in the state's courts proved on appeal either to be innocent or to have committed crimes meriting a lesser penalty. This made him place a moratorium on capital punishment in January 2000, and shortly afterwards to appoint a Commission to investigate it.

When Turow began work as a member of the Commission he was an agnostic about the death penalty. 'I still hung in a sort of ethical equilibrium,' he writes, 'afraid to come down on either side of the question of whether capital punishment was actually right or wise.' What he learned and saw as he served on the Commission made his mind up at last.

A book outlining the recent history of the death penalty in the United States, and the arguments and illustrative cases which weigh on either side of the debate about it, might seem to be one for lawyers and philosophers only. But Turow's account is a gripping read in the tradition of Truman Capote, anchored to realities, introducing the characters who played an important role in the Commission's work, and dramatising the factors pressing each side of the question. And drama it is; for the death penalty had almost fallen into abeyance in America by the 1960s, only to be revived in many states in the 70s. But moral and legal anxieties about its use caused many judges and states to restrict its application severely. A major factor in the increase of anxiety about capital punishment was the advent of DNA testing, which showed conclusively in many cases that the wrong man was sitting on death row.

Moreover, the lengthy, complex and multiply iterable appeals procedures in all states of the Union are such that a condemned prisoner can sit on death row for decades before being executed, released, or given a lesser sentence. The result is that the situation is a profoundly unsatisfactory one, and only in a very few states – a notable example is George W. Bush's Texas – has there lately been sufficient unconcern for the death penalty to be applied with any frequency.

Turow's book takes its readers fascinatingly through the history and the arguments, and concludes by outlining the Commission's recommendations. The Commission had not been asked whether the death penalty should be abolished, but how to make the monitoring and application of it less vulnerable to error. But the Commission members anyway recorded their view on that central and inescapable question, a majority saying that they were against capital punishment altogether. In true thriller style, Turow left to the very last word of the book his own answer to the question. But on the basis of what he had learned and seen, only one answer was possible.

History Lessons

Thucydides said that history is philosophy teaching by examples. He should have said, 'trying to teach by examples', because although the past provides our only data for navigating the future, we often fail to use it well – for two reasons: we miss the real point of its lessons, or we follow the wrong precedents. This latter is illustrated by those early prognosticators who thought that because triplanes flew better than biplanes, future aircraft would have twelve wings.

Consider the event that triggered the American civil rights movement. On 17 May 1954 the US Supreme Court found in favour of a black girl, Linda Brown, whose father had sued the Kansas Board of Education for refusing to admit her to an all-white local school, obliging her to commute to a run-down alternative an hour's journey from her home. Their judgment was the first crack in the US's 'Jim Crow' apartheid laws. Twenty years of bitter struggle later, the civil rights movement had climbed the mountain and seen the view: by then nearly half of all black children attended schools in which the majority of pupils were white.

By the logic of that process one would expect that by the beginning of the following century, thirty further years on, US education would be fully integrated. Alas, it was not. As the twenty-first century dawned, 70 per cent of black American children attended schools where the majority of students belonged to ethnic minorities. White segregationism had taken an alternative route: where once it used Jim Crow laws, it now used self-perpetuating income differentials to educate its children at private all-white schools whose alumni started with several large advantages over those who attended state-funded schools in poorer neighbourhoods, a cycle that can only therefore keep going when they have children of their own.

Are things any different in Britain? In London, and on a smaller scale everywhere else, not much. The reasons are not primarily racist, but an expression of the duty parents feel to do the best for their children, often with considerable burden to themselves, and even though they recognise that their choice maintains and even exacerbates a bad situation. But who would sacrifice a child's education in the interest of a general principle? If everyone did, it would not be the less good option they chose; but the fact is that people act on the basis of individual interests, afraid that in pursuit of general advantage they inflict particular disadvantage on their own.

The Brown ruling of 1954 was not, though, entirely a Pyrrhic victory. It started a process which helped reduce, although it did not efface, racial divisions. But it also entrenched a process in which wealth divisions maintained too much of the *de facto* outcome of racial divisions.

Another and seemingly opposite lesson offered by history, also always ambiguously learned, is that the bitterest rivalries are those between people who are close to one another in geographical, ethnic or religious respects, rather than between those who differ widely in all respects. Again consider: in which major monotheistic religion of Middle Eastern origin are men and women segregated, the latter required to conceal their hair, male infants circumcised, pork regarded as unclean, prayers offered several times a day, and Fridays kept holy? Is it Judaism or Islam? The answer is both (in their conservative manifestations). Which of the two arose among the Semitic peoples of the Middle East? The answer again is both. How different are languages in which the words for 'peace' are respectively *shalom* and *salaam*? And are these peoples friends or enemies?

The answer is yet again: both. Because the media thrive

almost exclusively on stories of conflict, little is heard about the many positive daily contacts between Israelis and Palestinians: the personal friendships, the peace movements on both sides, the mutual human-rights groups, and the thriving businesses staffed by Israeli and Palestinian co-workers. As with most conflicts, it is the extremist minorities on either side who make life intolerable for everyone else – the Israeli religious right who support Jewish settlement in the occupied territories, Hamas with its avowed policy of extirpating Israel altogether.

When Linda Brown went to third grade in Topeka, Kansas, she lived in the same land, spoke the same tongue, shared the same faith and had the same hopes as the whites who wished to exclude her. Perhaps history's point is that we must attend to the small differences among what is mostly shared, for they make the largest divisions when they get out of hand.

Identity

In politics, dogs are more often wagged by their tails than vice versa. Demonstrating this fact to perfection, reactionary-minded politicians of all parties are quick to espouse the idea of identity cards when one or another crisis of crime, terrorism or illegal immigration occurs, claiming their necessity in the war on all three. Thus, scores of millions of us in Britain (all, save the pure-bred of Wales and Cornwall, descended from illegal immigrants during the last two millennia) are periodically threatened with having to carry identity cards because some thousands of folk are here without the government's permission, or a dozen or so – at most – among us plan to kill unsuspecting civilians with a bomb.

The arguments against identity cards are too good and too well known to need rehearsing. They were compulsory during two world wars, but Churchill rightly abolished them after the second one, and no government since has felt able to justify their reintroduction. One among many reasons is that free people pride themselves on their liberties, and free citizens do not agree that the existence of a relatively small percentage of malefactors in their midst should oblige everyone else to undergo the nuisance and insult of having to carry identity papers for the police to look at whenever they wish.

But the question that talk of identity cards begs (in the correct sense of: assumes has already been answered) is an important one. What is an identity? Kenneth Williams once remarked that people who recognised him in the street were apt to point and say, 'Oh! do you know who *you* are!', reinforcing his uneasy sense that, in fact, he did not in the slightest know who he was. He thereby showed awareness of the two problems that infect concepts of identity. One is the question of what sort of person one really is (some people pay psychoanalysts a fortune to help them find out). The other concerns identity over time: in what sense, if any, is anyone the same person aged fifty that he was at twenty?

Both problems are complicated by the fact that no one is just one person. The various versions of Fred known to his parents, his wife, his colleagues, his friends and his dentist might inhabit the same body and live at the same address, but they can each cause surprises if encountered by the wrong audience. This is not a claim that Fred suffers 'multiple personality disorder', which is characterised by lack of integration between personalities housed within a single individual. Rather, it captures the way different aspects of Fred combine to offer different faces to others, or make him play different roles for them. The variety exhibited by his personae results from their being the product of his responses to others, individually tailored to the nature of each relationship.

Of course certain traits persist across personae, and these are what people well acquainted with him think is the 'real' Fred. But would Fred agree? There is quite likely to be yet another Fred – the inner, private, wishful, regretful, somewhat insecure but sometimes determined Fred who occasionally tells himself the truth and often deceives himself, and who dreams about playing for England and winning the lottery.

Overturning the long-held belief that an immortal soul is the basis of personal continuity over time, John Locke argued that identity is a function of memory. If at forty I am 'conscious to myself' of being the same person as I was at twenty, he said, then I am that same person; and if I do not, then I am not. 'Person' has a definite legal and moral meaning, as the entity to which rights attach and responsibilities belong.

This theory has some inconvenient consequences. One is that

if I lend you a fiver now, and you have a poor memory, what can I expect to get back in a year's time? Two pounds, if you vaguely remember the loan? Or nothing, if you have forgotten it – for why, without separate reason, should one person repay another's debts? Hereby hangs a long and curly philosophical tale.

'If you cannot resolve what you are,' said Martial, 'at last you will be nothing.' That reflection explains a long tradition in philosophy of encouraging the search for self-knowledge and self-creation. One obstacle is that the world always tries to mould us into shapes convenient for itself, since individuality is disruptive. It succeeds by rewarding conformity, from fashion to opinion, and by penalising those who will not concur. But it fails often enough for true individuality to survive, keeping hopes for originality and fresh beginnings alive.

Mass Values

In a frank, old-fashioned, unapologetic, utterly refreshing attack on the debasement of public sensibility by the mass media, Richard Hoggart in his *Mass Media in a Mass Society* showed how much he agrees with the great Lord Reith, whom he quotes: 'To apply [broadcasting] to the dissemination of the shoddy, the vulgar and the sensational would be a blasphemy against human nature.' Reith undoubtedly started revolving in his grave a long time ago, for there is little left in the popular media that is not tainted by vulgarity and sensationalism, and sometimes even shoddiness. In opposing this Hoggart pulled no punches in expressing bluffly aspirational Reithian attitudes towards what is necessary for the health of the public mind.

There is nothing in Hoggart's argument which is not achingly familiar to anyone who shares his outlook, but this is not a criticism, because the views he iterated are ones that both need and bear infinite iteration. He preached the moral, reflective, educated society. He preached standards, civility, imagination, awareness. He preached the democratic intelligence, the culturally enriched individual, the common good pitched high.

At every point in his analysis of what the mass media have done to the way people think, choose and act, he (and as a representative man, therefore, all those who think like him) can be accused of elitism and its supposed attendant vices of condescension, paternalism and the like. But the fact is that Hoggart is a prophet from a distinctive tradition in British culture: the tradition of the Workers' Educational Association, of night schools in industrial towns, of the autodidact consciousness. In nineteenth-century Britain an increase in literacy opened doors for mill workers, farmhands, domestic servants, shop assistants and cobblers to read the classics and discover the world and their rights. It is a tale that explains Hoggart (and was beautifully told by Jonathan Rose in his *The Intellectual Life of the British Working Class*), and by itself rebuts any charges of elitism and condescension. For it shows that Hoggart knew whereof he preached: that educating the judgement and sensibilities of individuals is what has a better chance than anything else of making a good society.

Hoggart's aim was to diagnose the changes that have taken place in society, and especially the contribution made by the mass media to that change, and then to propose remedies. The changes in question include, familiarly, increasing wealth and advancing technology, along with declining religious belief and democratic participation. Conjoin these with what Hoggart described as 'under-education' and the result is a divided, coarsened, consumption-besotted society whose guides and servants, the popular mass media, massively reinforce these negatives in their own pursuit of profit, abdicating any responsibility even of a faintly Reithian kind to inform, educate, challenge and inspire. There are positive aspects to the new dispensation, Hoggart acknowledged, chief among them the greater degree of personal freedom available to the majority of us. But we do not put it to anything like good enough use, most noticeably by not using it to combat the negatives listed.

In just the way that this Jeremiad strikes well-known notes, so do the remedies Hoggart proposed; but here he was briefer, vaguer and less convincing, except in one particular. We need more democracy, and more scope for charities and public do-good bodies, Hoggart said; and we need to help the underclass, improve comprehensive schools, improve general nutrition – and so on. He was and remains of course right, but (also of course) who could disagree? and do we not anyway always try, at least with most of these things?

The one particular in which Hoggart said something unfashionably suggestive concerns the role of 'the intellectual' in the leavening of the social loaf. He reminded his readers that the British reflex is to shy away from the very word, let alone the idea, and even more the thing itself, as pretentious at best, useless mainly, and dangerous at worst. And this is done mostly by intellectuals themselves, who disavow any responsibility for engaging with, advising, educating or challenging the public mind, and who deflect with irony and a faint wry smile any suggestion to the contrary. But the flippant style and even the faux downmarket tastes (watching demotic television with sarcastic relish) are a disguise – probably of anxiety, though Hoggart's charge was stronger: it was one of dereliction of duty. The obscure Judes and hopeful Leonard Basts of this world, struggling to improve themselves, need – he said – their help.

Thus Hoggart iterated some old but true, obvious but good, familiar but important ideas. Their iteration is well worthwhile.

People

Plato
427–347 BC

A. N. Whitehead famously remarked that Western philosophy is a series of footnotes to Plato. There is a large measure of truth in this remark, for most of the major themes of Western philosophy are addressed – sometimes fully and sometimes at least by suggestion – in Plato's writings, which embrace metaphysics (which asks: what is the ultimate nature of reality?), epistemology (which asks: what is knowledge and how do we get it?), ethics (which asks: what is good and how should we live accordingly?), politics (which asks: what is the best form of society?), and aesthetics (which asks: what is art, and what is beauty?).

Along the way Plato had much to suggest about aspects of logic and philosophical method too, partly in the form of remarks on reason and argument, but more by his actual practice – exemplified by the Socratic dialogue – of a forensic style of enquiry involving critical discussion, examination of concepts, conjecture and refutation, and an unremitting search for clarity.

As these observations imply, the Western philosophical tradition owes a great deal of its matter and form to Plato. And as if this were not already enough, the writings in which he conveyed this matter and form are works of the highest literary quality. He was, in short, a genius, and there are very few like him anywhere in history.

This unquestionable fact about Plato should neither obscure, nor be taken to recommend, those aspects of his views which are arguably wrong or disagreeable. For a major example: his ideal state is an authoritarian one in which children are bred according to eugenic principles – their parents selected and mated on grounds of appearance and intelligence – and then brought up in communal orphanages and assigned to roles in life suitable to their capacities. The state makes all these decisions. Its rulers are to be philosophers, celibate and propertyless (and therefore, in theory, disinterested), living collegially and brooking no opposition. The vision is implicitly of a fascist Utopia, and part of its inspiration is that Plato, who was an aristocrat by descent, hated the Athenian democracy which had put his teacher Socrates to death, and which had led Athens to its disastrous defeat in the Peloponnesian War against Sparta. These two painful events overshadowed Plato's early life, and have to be remembered in any account of the development of his views.

But even an unblinking recognition of these considerations does not diminish the enormous achievement of Plato's thought. The Oxford philosopher Gilbert Ryle once speculated that Plato did not at first have major ambitions in philosophy, but desired instead a purely literary reputation. He entered his dialogues for competition at the Games – as this indicates, the antique Games were not limited to athletics – and only turned to serious philosophical endeavour later, when the seriousness of the questions he had been writing about began to impress him.

Whether or not this picture is accurate, it is certainly true that the dialogues assigned to the early period of Plato's creative life – the *Laches*, *Ion*, *Charmides* and a number of others – are relatively slight in philosophical content, and almost invariably end without a solution to the problems they address, as if their display of forensic and rhetorical skill were what really mattered. But some of them, perhaps those written towards the end of that period, such as the *Apology*, *Gorgias* and *Protagoras*, have greater depth; and by the time of the important dialogues *Meno* and especially *Republic* (Plato's most famous work), it is no longer in doubt whether Plato was earnest about the problems under discussion.

All of Plato's most important dialogues appeared in his 'middle' period – together with the *Meno* and *Republic* they are *Cratylus, Phaedo, Symposium, Phaedrus, Parmenides* and *Theaetetus*. They jointly state, and in the case especially of the last two they profoundly self-criticise, Plato's mature philosophical views. The dialogues of his 'late' period (*Sophist, Statesman, Laws, Philebus, Critias* and *Timaeus* – this last the only one known in Europe during the Dark and Middle Ages) have little influence on characterisations of the middle-period views, which are regarded as most distinctively Platonic.

One way to give a summary description of these views is to start with Plato's theory of knowledge. Knowledge, Plato held, is about what is eternally and immutably true. Any object of knowledge must likewise be something perfect, permanent and unchanging. Since everything in the world of our ordinary experience is just the opposite, it follows that we never have knowledge of them, but at best only beliefs or opinions. Nor can we, with our inadequate capacities, extrapolate from the things of ordinary life to perfect and eternal things in any other realm. How then do we ever come to have knowledge?

The answer, said Plato, is that we have immortal souls which, before being embodied, were in contact with the perfect and eternal objects of knowledge in what Plato called 'the realm of Being', so called because things truly exist there. (In the ordinary world, which Plato called the 'realm of Becoming' because everything is changing – i.e. becoming something else – things exist only in an incomplete sense, courtesy of their 'participation in' the truly existing entities of the realm of Being). When our immortal souls enter a physical body – and because they are immortal they do this repeatedly – they forget all they knew. The process of education is therefore not one of being taught, but of being reminded, of some of the realm of Being's eternal verities.

In this sketch one sees not just Plato's theory of knowledge but also his metaphysics – that is, his account of the true nature of the world as a dual realm, and of human beings as a union between immortal, reincarnated souls and forgetful, limiting bodies. From these premises his ethical and political views follow. Those truly existing entities in the realm of Being, the 'Forms', are the perfect exemplars of their kind. It is by 'participating in' or by resembling (the difference is great, and Plato criticised his own inability to resolve it) its Form that anything in the ordinary world is what it is. Thus, an act is good if it participates in the 'Form of the Good'; moral action consists in striving to know that Form, for, as soon as one does, one can no longer do wrong. Virtue is knowledge, wrong-doing is the result of ignorance.

In the *Republic* Plato gave a parallel account of the good man and the good state, treating each as an analogy of the other. His key concept is 'justice', meaning balance or well-orderedness between the elements of the state – or, internally, of the individual soul. In arguing for harmony as the pivotal notion in both spheres, Plato expresses one of the most characteristic and central of classical Greek ideals.

Until his late period Plato invariably used Socrates as the principal mouthpiece in his dialogues. Some conjecture that the early dialogues are faithful representations of Socrates' views and his methods, but that as Plato's own views developed, as expressed in the middle dialogues, so Socrates reduces to a mere spokesman. The suggestion is plausible. Whatever the extent of Socrates' influence, it is Plato's middle dialogues – the truly Platonic ones – which contain the germs of Western thought, and for which his genius is chiefly remembered and applauded.

Aristotle
384–322 BC

When learning revived in the Middle Ages, prompting the growth of scholarly monasteries and universities, and especially as these latter grew in importance in the western kingdoms of Christian Europe, the single most dominating influence in the intellectual life of the time was Aristotle. The great project of medieval philosophy – the philosophy of the Schools, known as Scholastic philosophy – was to reconcile the teachings of Aristotle, who was known simply as 'The Philosopher', with the Christian scriptures. In almost every aspect of Scholastic thought the presence of Aristotle was felt, to such an extent that the first 'modern' philosophers – Descartes, Locke and others in the seventeenth century – had to struggle to free themselves from Aristotelian influence in order to make their own contributions.

The largest part of the reason for Aristotle's longstanding dominance of philosophy is the sheer range of his work. It covers practically the whole extent of human enquiry, from logic, metaphysics and ethics to psychology and biology, taking in politics and aesthetics on the way. The works of Aristotle that remain to us are his lecture notes – the dialogues he wrote, in the fashion of his teacher Plato, have all been lost. The profundity and originality of Aristotle's writings make them supreme documents of the Western tradition. Several still form a central part of the philosophy curriculum in today's universities.

One of Aristotle's works continues to form a central part of an even more extensive and indeed vital debate, namely ethics, the question about the best life for humankind. His great classic, the *Nicomachean Ethics*, is one of the indispensable works of ethical literature. It is the first work ever to offer a systematic ethical theory. Despite being a philosophical treatise, it is marvellously readable and stimulating.

Ordinary folk, Aristotle observes, value pleasure, businessmen value wealth, and gentlemen value honour, but each of these is merely instrumental to a higher good, which by common consent is: happiness. The task of ethics is to describe the true nature of happiness, and to say how to attain it. This is what the *Nicomachean Ethics* is about.

In identifying happiness as the supreme good Aristotle had a particular concept of it in mind, which he called *eudaimonia*, a word that denotes an active state of well-being and well-doing. People choose *eudaimonia* as the chief goal, Aristotle says, because it is complete and sufficient in itself, not merely a means to something better; and this self-sufficiency and completeness of the highest good is what man, as a rational being, properly seeks.

The point about rationality is central. It is man's defining mark, his essence. Since the good life for man is life in accordance with his essence, the rational life – the life of 'practical wisdom' – is best; for it is life lived 'in accordance with virtue'.

By 'virtue' Aristotle meant what a rational person will choose as the middle path or 'mean' between opposing vices. Thus courage is the mean between cowardice and rashness, generosity is the mean between miserliness and profligacy. Following the mean is not quite 'moderation' in the ordinary sense, for Aristotle's virtuous man is not simply a continent one, given that a life of practical wisdom will always allow appropriate expression of needs and appetites in their due place.

An attractive feature of Aristotle's view is that it does not turn on a list of 'dos' and 'don'ts' but instead requires that each situation be wisely treated on its merits. If you cannot be wise, says Aristotle, imitate those who are. Eventually you will learn how to be prudent; living the good life is a life-long project in which you can grow.

And Aristotle was alert to the difficulties in doing this. Plato had argued that people only do wrong out of ignorance. This seems implausible, for surely people sometimes know what is right yet still do wrong for many reasons, chief among them weakness of will. Aristotle's theory makes room for this latter, diagnosing it as a contest between rational choice and non-rational desire, won by the latter.

The rational person who attains *eudaimonia* is described by Aristotle as 'magnanimous', which means 'having a great soul'. The magnanimous man is the original model of the 'gentleman' where this term is not understood in a social sense, but in the sense of a man whose way of acting and being is distinctively considerate and reflective.

A famous section of the *Nicomachean Ethics* discusses friendship, which in Aristotle's view is one of the greatest goods. He distinguishes genuine friendships from those based merely on mutual pleasure or usefulness. These last only as long as what they offer, whereas true friendship is permanent because 'grounded in good'. A friend is 'another self', and therefore merits the kind of concern we have for ourselves. Self-concern is appropriate for an ethical individual, who will be motivated by it to act nobly and live intelligently. In seeing what is best for himself he will thereby see what is best for his friend.

But the highest ideal of the good is reserved by Aristotle for the life of contemplation. It is easy to see why: if reason is man's essence, its pure disinterested exercise is man's essential activity. The contemplative life must therefore attract the greatest possible happiness. Aristotle wrote, 'The rule is that what is best and most pleasant for each creature is what intimately belongs to it. In applying that rule to man we see that the life of the intellect is best and most pleasant for him, because the intellect more than anything else *is* the man. So the life of the intellect will be the happiest life for man.'

If the contemplative life is best, what should be contemplated? Aristotle's answer is 'eternal truths'. This is the philosopher's vocation, and Aristotle concedes that it is not to everyone's taste, nor within everyone's grasp. This means that the very best life is open only to a few: those with the requisite intelligence, and enough wealth to give them leisure to use it.

Some complain that this is elitism, and means that ordinary people are excluded from *eudaimonia*. The criticism has force, and Aristotle himself conceded that luck helps some to live the best life. But most of what he says applies generally, not least his views on justice. He defines doing injustice as getting more than one ought, and suffering injustice as getting less than one ought; and therefore justice is equity – to deal justly is to do what is fair. This applies irrespectively of social status or moral luck.

There are significant defects in Aristotle's views. He lived in a society based on slavery, and not only saw nothing wrong with it but even held that some are naturally born to be slaves. Moreover, there is something of the complacent bourgeois about his ideal pursuer of the 'middle way', a character somewhat at odds with the purely contemplative philosopher. But the burgh of Aristotle's bourgeois was, remember, classical Athens; so for him there was no inconsistency. And these strictures take nothing away from the richness of ethical and psychological insight in his great classic, most of which remains highly relevant and instructive today.

Lucretius
c. 96–55 BC

Apart from his authorship of the literary and philosophical masterpiece *On the Nature of Things*, almost nothing is known about Lucretius, except that his full name was Titus Lucretius Carus and that he lived for about forty-five of the years between 100 and 50 BC. The literary merits of Lucretius' majestic poem were appreciated and admired by his contemporaries; its philosophical merits continue to be appreciated to the present day, not only because it is the chief source of information about the philosophy of Epicurus, but because it influenced a number of major figures in the Western tradition, among them Gassendi, Bergson, Santayana and Whitehead. Through Gassendi the poem spurred the revival of atomism, and thereby contributed to the rise of modern science.

Lucretius' poem is a statement, and in several respects a development, of the views of a philosopher who lived two centuries before his own time, and whom he passionately admired: Epicurus. Epicurus' system is naturalistic; it says that reality consists of material atoms interacting in a void, thus giving rise to all the phenomena of the universe, including man and his perceptions and sentiments. The aim of the theory is not restricted to describing how reality is built out of material particles on mechanical principles, but has an ethical aim based on this naturalistic physics: the aim of liberating mankind from superstition and ignorance. In particular, said Epicurus, by being helped to understand the true nature of the world, people will be freed from the worst of all fears, the fear of death. If the world is a material realm of which man is a natural part, subject only to natural laws, then the processes of coming into and going out of existence are natural and simple, and apply to everything in nature. And nothing natural, Epicurus said, can hold any terrors.

In Epicurus' view, the good for man is pleasure, by which he principally meant friendship and the study of philosophy – not the eating, drinking and merrymaking connoted by the modern sense of the term 'epicure'. What most think of as pleasure-giving – indulgence of various kinds – is in fact a source of pain, as the example of (say) a hangover illustrates. Epicurus' ethical outlook can be encapsulated in the advice to pursue pleasure and to avoid pain, where 'pleasure' and 'pain' are understood in the special rather ascetic senses he attached to them.

Lucretius believed passionately in the Epicurean project of liberating mankind from fear through understanding the true nature of the world, and this is what his great poem addresses. The poem is an epic in six books, the last of which is unfinished. The first two books set out Epicurus' physics of atoms and the void, and the third book applies his physics to the question of mind. Since the mind is a material function of the body, it is mortal just as the body is, and ceases to exist when the body dies. This is the fact which does most to free us from fear of death, says Lucretius: in his famous words, '*nil igitur mors est ad nos*' – 'death therefore is nothing to us' – for being dead is no more or less than being unborn.

The poem's fourth book discusses perception, and ends with another famous Lucretian foray, namely his attack on sexual infatuation. (His remedy for the pains of 'falling in love' is promiscuity, which, he in effect says, will save you from the trap of becoming besotted with one person, a situation in which tranquillity is impossible, being full of pains and fears). In the fifth book, an account of the development both of life on earth and of civilisations, Lucretius anticipates evolutionary theories about the appearance and extinction of plants and animals. And finally, his incomplete sixth book addresses such phenomena as storms, volcanoes and plagues, including the terrible Athenian plague of 430 BC.

What adds poignancy to the courageous naturalism of Lucretius' Epicureanism is the fact that he lived through an especially dangerous time in Roman history. His half of the first century BC saw repeated civil wars, the bloody dictatorship of Sulla, the great slave revolt under Spartacus with its ghastly outcome – the bodies of thousands of crucified rebels lining the Appian Way – the Catilinian conspiracy with the scandals, intrigues and upheavals it caused; and of course, in the years close to the time of Lucretius' death, the death of the Roman Republic itself, killed by these disasters. In championing the Epicurean view with such passion and conviction, Lucretius was offering a way of living designed to protect people from the insecurity of the times.

In addition to its importance as the only detailed statement of Epicurean philosophy – there would otherwise only be a few surviving fragments of Epicurus' own writings, and the references (often hostile) in early commentators – Lucretius' poem is equally important for its literary excellence. Cicero praised it as 'rich in brilliant genius and high artistry', even though he was unsympathetic to its tenets; and it provided a model and a source of inspiration to Virgil, who alludes admiringly to it in his 'Georgics'. There is extraordinary beauty in the poem, especially when Lucretius talks of the countryside, which he obviously loved and knew well, and in many of the comments on life there is deep feeling exquisitely expressed, the result of reflection on experience married to literary craftsmanship of the highest order.

Such information as can be culled from the poem suggests that Lucretius was a member of the aristocratic clan of the Lucretii, and was highly educated. Both snippets are of much significance, given the paucity of biographical data otherwise. Slaves owned by members of the Lucretii would have called themselves by the clan name too, but Lucretius addresses his aristocratic dedicatee Gaius Memmius as an equal and a friend, and it is clear that he was superbly educated, knowing Greek and philosophy, and having an exceptional mastery of his own tongue besides. His atheism and materialism made him unpopular with later Christian writers, one of whom, St Jerome, claimed that he was mad, and wrote his poem during occasional intervals of lucidity. Jerome also says that Lucretius killed himself by drinking a love potion, an improbable idea given the poet's emphatic strictures on infatuation. The imputation of madness hardly seems to apply to one who could say, as Lucretius did in summing up the message he wished to convey from Epicurus' teaching:

> O wretched minds of men! O hearts so blind!
> How dark the life, how great the perils are
> In which whatever time is given is passed!
> Do you not see that nature cries for this,
> And only this, that pain from out the body
> Shall be removed away, and mind enjoy
> Sweet sense of pleasure, freed from care and fear?
>
> Book 2, lines 11–19 in Latin

The desire to bring intellectual and moral freedom through knowledge of nature is a noble one, and Lucretius' expression of it gave us a work which is both a philosophical and a literary classic. In being both these things simultaneously his great poem stands almost alone in world literature, and still has its power to amuse, amaze, instruct and inspire.

Cicero
106–43 BC

To appreciate Cicero properly one should view him through the lens of admiration supplied by those distinguished figures in periods of enlightenment – the Renaissance and the eighteenth century especially – who learned much from him, who enjoyed his famously beautiful Latin, and who – above all – valued his humanism. The great David Hume, in a letter to Frances Hutcheson, described Cicero as his favourite author on moral questions. Earlier, the equally great Erasmus said that whenever he read Cicero's *On Old Age*, he felt like kissing the book, and that the noble Roman should be called 'St Cicero'.

Earlier still, Cicero was Petrarch's best-loved author, and both Petrarch and his Renaissance successors were enchanted by his style, to the extent that some swore they would never use any Latin expression not found in his writings. Such was the hunger to write pure Latin in the Renaissance world that Ciceronian forms and mannerisms invaded even theological writing, to the extent that some churchman went so far as to call God 'Jupiter'.

But what the Renaissance chiefly valued in Cicero was his belief in the human realm and human values. He was, in short, a humanist in the modern sense of the term – that is, one who believes that identifying the good for mankind can only be done by understanding human needs, interests and desires. He believed that individuals are autonomous, free to think and choose for themselves; and that they have rights, and that rights imply responsibilities. Above all he believed that all men are brothers; 'There is nothing so like anything else as we are to one another,' he wrote, adding that 'kindness, generosity, goodness and justice' are the deepest ties holding the human community together. He based this view on a fundamental premise: that each of us possesses a divine spark of reason, and that this fact requires us to develop ourselves to the fullest extent possible as civilised, informed, reflective individuals.

Cicero's Renaissance admirers knew that he had advanced these views during a tumultuous and often terrible period in Rome's history – the last years of the Republic, as it collapsed into a civil war that culminated first in Julius Caesar's dictatorship and then, after further struggles, in the empire established by Augustus. Cicero saw all forms of autocracy as slavery; he quitted Rome for his estate in Tusculum, when Caesar became dictator and there, in the short space of a few months, wrote his best and most enduring works, among them the *Tusculan Disputations*, *On Duty* and *On Friendship*.

Cicero was an educated and thoughtful man who, despite his major role in the legal and political affairs of Rome, remained a lifelong student of Greek philosophy. His aim, when at last the opportunity of leisure arrived, was to offer the fruits of Greek thought to his Roman contemporaries in accessible form. This would now be called 'popularising', and much later – among modern scholars who charged Cicero with 'unoriginality' and 'derivativeness' – this was held against him. But he was consciously modest in his aims; he did not wish to reproduce the technicality and rigour of the Greeks, given that those features of their thought can be of interest only to scholars. His desire was to convey what was useful to the practice of living, and to disseminate the best ideas of the Greek thinkers to that end. This does not mean that he was incapable of getting down to logical niceties himself; his *Academics* and *The Nature of the Gods* show otherwise.

But although Cicero's primary aim was to popularise, he was

no mere transmitter. He was an intelligent and perceptive adapter, who selected ideas and wove them together, in elegant and beautiful form, according to his own extensive experience of life and the mature judgements it helped him make. As history has proved, he succeeded in doing this not just for his contemporaries, but for all reflective people in all succeeding time.

Cicero had admirers even before the Renaissance, though his medieval readers were nervously conscious that his writings had been proscribed by Pope Gregory I (590–604) on the grounds that their beautiful style and beguiling interest were too likely to distract young men from the study of scripture. Even so, medieval philosophy owed much of its technical terminology to Cicero, who in adapting from Greek had given careful thought to technical terms. We accordingly owe him, by the usual route of lexical migration from Latin, the English words *appetite, comprehension, definition, difference, element, image, individual, induction, infinity, instance, notion, morality, property, quality, science, species, vacuum*, and many more.

It was not of course just the words, but the ideas they conveyed, which enriched the Western mind. Dante acknowledged his debt to Cicero in many respects: for example, to Cicero's *On Duties* for the list of sins in the *Inferno*, and to Cicero's *Dream of Scipio* for the very idea of an educational journey through hell, purgatory and heaven. In the light of such influence, it is scarcely surprising that the new world of the Renaissance should find Cicero an inspiration in general.

Petrarch at first cited Cicero as the model of a man who makes active use of a quiet and private life to cultivate his mind. He then discovered that Cicero had lived instead a vigorous and sometimes perilous public life. This aspect of Cicero – and chiefly his belief in public duty – recommended itself greatly to the Renaissance. The refined, civilised man who divides his time between public engagement in affairs and private intellectual refinement came to be called a 'Renaissance man', but 'Ciceronian' would be an equally fitting term.

Cicero's works became best-sellers in the Renaissance period, and have remained so for most of history since. They were among the first to pour in numbers from the newly invented printing presses of the mid-fifteenth century, a technological innovation which helped spread his influence even further. His writings became standard texts in schools, especially *On Duties* and the *Tusculan Disputations*. When Hume told Frances Hutcheson, in the letter already quoted, that Cicero was his favourite moral author, he added that his least favourite book had been a Protestant tract called *The Whole Duty of Man*, a staple for school children of his day. The implication was that he, like many thoughtful votaries of all enlightenments since Cicero's time, had been rescued by Cicero's civilised, urbane humanism. The sentiment has been repeated many times in the intellectual history of the West.

Later scholars, beginning with that nineteenth-century doyen of classical studies Theodore Mommsen, disdained Cicero because they viewed him as a 'mere' syncretist and populariser. This does him no justice. Neither Hume nor Petrarch, neither Erasmus nor Dante, indeed no humanist of the Renaissance or Enlightenment, would have been able to understand such a limited view of a figure whose graces of style and thought gave them and the Western mind so much.

Seneca
3 BC–AD 65

S eneca is a valuable figure in the history of Western culture
in at least two ways. He is our earliest full source of information about Stoic ethics, and he is the author of agreeable,
instructive and perceptive essays on the philosophy of life. His
writings in this genre are a paradigm of their kind, deploying
argument and the lessons of experience to advance Stoicism's
commitment to a life of self-control, responsibility, and harmony with nature. His statement of the proper Stoic attitude
towards death – it occurs at the end of Book VI of his *Natural
Questions* – is perhaps the most brilliant and persuasive ever
written; but it is not alone in conveying the rich insights of
Seneca's mature intelligence. The *Moral Letters to Lucilius* are
a treasury of these reflections, and they have the added charm
that in each of them Seneca also reports an idea he finds valuable
in the writings of other philosophers, eclectically welcoming
anything which can help a reflective individual live a better life.

Seneca's moral letters and other works were as widely admired
in the Renaissance as in his own day. Elizabeth I of England
translated his writings for her own instruction, finding them
'full of good advisings'. In the late Renaissance and early modern
period his dramas were even more influential than his ethical
writings. It is an interesting question how far Seneca's plays
provided instruction to Shakespeare, but his role as a teacher of
morality almost certainly had a part in inspiring several of the
moralists who figure in Shakespeare's *oeuvre*, from Jacques and

Gonzalo to Polonius. But this thought touches another side of Seneca's later reputation too; for some came to see him – unfairly, and doubtlessly on too little acquaintance either with the content of his ethical thinking or with his achievements as a statesman – as a prosing, moralising bore.

This aspect of Seneca's reputation is partly to be explained by the fact that the taste and attitudes of later generations are often crucially influenced by a person's near contemporaries. The grammarian and rhetorician Fronto, who taught Stoic philosophy to Marcus Aurelius a century after Seneca's time, disliked the latter's writings because of their version of the Silver Age style. Seneca takes to an advanced degree the Silver Age's taste for aphoristic compression, to such an extent that even much later critics, for a chief instance Lord Macaulay, objected that every one of Seneca's sentences could be a quotation or motto, and that reading him was therefore (as Macaulay put it) like permanently having nothing besides anchovies to eat.

Fronto also complained that, because of his delight in finding pithy ways of expressing his insights, Seneca was apt to repeat the same thought too many times even in the same passage. For Fronto as for many later readers, the best Latin model for philosophical writing was provided not by Seneca but by Cicero, who patterned himself more closely on his Greek originals.

These strictures are not without force. But two important points can be made in Seneca's defence. One is that each letter to Lucilius was intended to be taken as a separate and self-standing entity, rather like a weekly column in a newspaper today. If a columnist were to collect his articles into a single volume, and a reader were to try to go through them in one sitting, their similarity of technique might quickly make them pall. The other point is that Seneca seriously intended his presentation of the insights of Stoicism to be food for thought, so each one merited being mulled over and remembered – hence the pointed manner in which he stated them. Taken together, these points say that Seneca is to be read in small portions, a letter at a time, each allowed its due weight and impact; and when he is thus read, the best of what he offers becomes apparent.

It is a significant fact about Seneca that he was a man of affairs. He was, in effect, prime minister of the Roman empire for the first eight years of Nero's reign, a period admired and applauded by history (and by Seneca's own contemporaries and successors) for its peace, prosperity and good government. Seneca and his partner in government, the head of the Praetorian Guard Sextus Afranius Burrus, were able to rule with little interference from the young Nero, who had been Seneca's pupil. But when others who had Nero's ear began to influence him, the years of stability came to an end. Seneca saw the trouble brewing before it arrived, and asked Nero's permission to resign so that he could retire to study and write.

Seneca had learned what he required for his exemplary statesmanship from legal practice and ministerial responsibility in the preceding reign of Claudius, from travels to Egypt, and from his reading. He had been on the receiving end of political difficulties, as when he was twice condemned to death as a result of being caught between factions in the political quarrels of the Claudian period. The sentences were commuted to exile, and were bitter enough experiences, as one of his earlier letters (a letter not intended for publication) revealed. But true to his philosophical outlook Seneca learned from these experiences, and when he held power in his own turn he exercised it responsibly, offering a sharp contrast to his persecutors.

His philosophical outlook and his practice were not, however, always consistent – at least, so some of his critics argued. The main reason for their charge was that Seneca became very wealthy during his career, largely because of his banking activities (which is to say: he lent money at interest, thus attracting the once-odious accusation of 'usury'). Again there are two replies. One is that Stoicism did not outlaw wealth – on the contrary, it frankly acknowledged that it is easier to be good when well-supplied materially; what it argued was that one should still be able to be good without this advantage, particularly if one once had wealth but lost it. The other is that Seneca with equal frankness always acknowledged that he knew himself to fall far short of the precepts he urged in his writings: 'Not only am I not a perfect man,' he wrote, 'I am not even a tolerable one.' No charge of hypocrisy could stick unless he claimed the reverse.

If there is a test of Seneca's commitment to Stoic ideals, it is the manner of his death. Nero obliged him to commit suicide – a form of capital sentence accorded to senior Romans – following the failure of a conspiracy led by Piso, which Seneca was suspected of supporting. Seneca did not flinch, but accepted the inevitable with courage, leaving life while still in full possession of his intellectual power, and bequeathing to the world a body of moral reflection and insight which it would be far poorer without.

Marcus Aurelius
AD 121–180

Marcus Aurelius Antoninus (AD 121–180) was both a Roman emperor and a philosopher, a rare combination, and in its way a happy one; for he was one of a succession of emperors, the Antonines, who made the second century AD a Golden Age for imperial Rome. It was the century that saw Galen in medicine, Ptolemy in astronomy and Lucian in literature – and not least, Marcus Aurelius himself in philosophy. 'Golden Age' is Gibbon's description of the period; taking the longer view, the Antonine age might better be characterised as the Indian summer of the Roman Empire in the West, for after Marcus Aurelius's reign the Empire's decline and fall began in earnest. Indeed the auguries of this collapse were already present during Aurelius's reign, in the form of waves of barbarian aggression on the borders of the Empire, which the otherwise pacific and philosophical emperor had to spend arduous years defending. Some commentators fault Aurelius for not solving the problem, but a fairer view is that the second century was an era of mass migration and tribal restlessness along Rome's borders, pushing relentlessly against them and overstraining the Empire's military and economic resources. Aurelius, after the manner of Canute, was faced with a tide of history.

Aurelius's philosophy was largely drawn from Stoicism, one of the great schools of thought originating in the Hellenic age of Greece. While campaigning on the River Danube, the empire's northern border, Aurelius kept a notebook, in which he jotted down his thoughts in Greek, together with advice to himself and comments on how to live with fortitude and probity. He gave this miscellany the title 'To Myself'. When it was published after his death it was recognised as an *aureus libellus*, a 'golden book' or classic, and it has retained a reputation ever since as a graceful and noble homily on life. In English translation it is standardly known as *The Meditations*.

As a young man Aurelius was introduced by his tutor, the famous rhetorician Fronto, to the teachings of the Stoic philosopher Epictetus (*c*.50–*c*.120). This encounter made Aurelius a convinced and lifelong Stoic. The school of thought to which he thus gave allegiance had been founded by Zeno of Citium about 300 BC, and it was named after the Athenian *stoa*, or 'porch', where the early members of the school met. It became the most influential and widespread of the great philosophical schools of the Hellenic and Roman periods, developing powerful traditions in logic and metaphysics as well as ethics. It was, however, its ethical teachings which were the most important feature for the majority of its adherents. As a practical philosophy of life it received a full expression in the *Discourses* of Epictetus, and it was these that influenced Aurelius.

Epictetus was a Greek who had been brought as a slave to Rome to serve as a tutor in a patrician household. His pupil, Arrian, made careful notes of Epictetus's lectures and subsequently published them; these are the *Discourses* which are one of the principal sources of our knowledge of his thought, the other being the *Enchiridion*, a 'handbook' to his thought also compiled by Arrian.

Epictetus's central tenet is that we must distinguish between what lies within our power and what lies outside our power, learning how to master the former and to accept the latter with fortitude. Only our own emotions, thoughts and appetites – our inner mental life – are in our own power, so we should govern these while cultivating what came to be described as 'stoic indifference' to factors beyond our control. These latter included not only what the world and other people do to us, but some of the ungovernable facts of our nature, mainly those associated with pleasure and pain.

As a way of managing life according to this distinction, Epictetus taught that rational anticipation of what our actions and choices might result in, and firm self-government and an ordered life, will lead towards the well-lived life.

The lack of dogmatism in Epictetus meant that influences and ideas from other schools of thought found their resonances in his views. This open-mindedness was attractive to Aurelius, who found much to value in ideas outside the Stoic tradition; so although the main framework of his outlook is Stoic, he profited from his study of other schools, including that of Plato. Aurelius did not add to or develop Stoic ethics other than by making it hospitable to congenial influences, but he beautifully demonstrates its applicability and adaptability as a philosophy of life.

In the *Meditations* Aurelius expresses the view that the universe is an organic living unity, in which everything is related to everything else, and in which human individuals are 'limbs' of the whole. It follows that the well-being of individuals is dependent upon the well-being of everything else. In the same way, each individual is inseparably an organic part of his society, so that individual good cannot be detached from the good of the collective. People are essentially social creatures – using 'essential' here in its strong philosophical sense to mean that they cannot be otherwise – and this means that the growth, flourishing and achievement of the individual cannot take place other than in a social setting. By the same token, the well-being of society depends on that of its members: the collective's interests neither outweigh nor negate individual interests; it is simply that the two coexist in indissoluble union, and must be cherished together.

One of the great tenets of Stoicism from its beginnings is that whatever happens 'in accordance with nature' is for that very reason good, and that therefore the only bad things that can happen to people are the result of their own failings. It follows that when what we might ordinarily think of as a bad thing happens to a good person, it is not, from that person's perspective, really bad; indeed, nothing bad can happen to the good. Take the example of a disease: to the good person disease is simply a natural fact, and as such something to be accepted with equanimity. People who do bad things should not be punished but taught, for as soon as they understand what is good they will do it. In this optimistic (and at least debatable) view Aurelius follows the teaching of Socrates as Plato presents it; in the view of both Socrates and Aurelius, everyone is seeking their own good, and if they do wrong it is because they are ignorant of the right way.

The most Socratic of Aurelius's views is that the good life is one based on reflection and self-examination. By these means we come to the self-government enjoined by Epictetus and the whole Stoic tradition, and thereby happiness. One of the themes that best exemplifies Aurelius's commitment to this thesis is his view on death. Human life is a small matter in the great cosmos, he says, and its cycles of life, change and death are natural and inevitable. We should therefore see our own deaths as no more than that – natural and inevitable, good because natural, nothing to fear, and indeed not even very important as measured against the great scheme of things. If we base our beliefs in a rational manner on what we know to be inevitable, we will suffer neither fear nor anguish.

The Stoic view is a courageous one, and Aurelius's version of it adds to it a quiet but profound dignity. Of course there is much to question in it, not least what some might see as the Stoic's self-anaesthetisation against what more sensitive and appetitive souls will see as the ecstasies and heights of love, passion, experience of the arts, even of terror and despair as creatively fruitful experiences in their own right. No Stoic could accept the idea that excess and psychological risk can be, or can lead to, good, yet one can imagine strong arguments showing that they are wrong. Nevertheless, for many aspects of life, and for many phases of life, the quiet courage and deep tranquillity afforded by Stoicism's noble outlook, not least in Aurelius's beautiful rendering of it, have much to offer, as readers of his pages invariably find.

Heloise and Abelard
Heloise, AD 1101–1164
Abelard, AD 1079–1142

A s one of the most famous couples in the annals of passion, Abelard and Heloise are invariably listed in that order: 'Abelard and Heloise'. To write instead 'Heloise and Abelard' is to make a large and appropriate statement; for it is Heloise who is first in the story of their passion, being the one with the truly eloquent heart, to her very core the paradigm of a woman whose love is so profound that it rejects and defies the whole world and the wrath of God – everything, indeed, other than the beloved himself.

The story is familiar in outline because it is iconic. Abelard, the brilliant young philosopher, had an affair with Heloise, the gifted and intelligent niece of a canon of Notre Dame in Paris, in whose house both she and Abelard lodged. Abelard began as her tutor, but they quickly became lovers. Their wildly erotic passion resulted in her pregnancy and the birth of a son, whom they called Astralabe. The couple married secretly, but Heloise's uncle, incensed by Abelard, had a gang of thugs attack him and brutally castrate him. The attack and the attendant scandal forced Abelard into a monastery and Heloise (at Abelard's bidding but with terrible reluctance) into a convent.

The prominence of the couple in twelfth-century Paris might have caused the scandal of their love to leave traces in history even if they had not later engaged in their famous correspondence, because Abelard was the leading thinker of the day, a proud and contentious figure who made many enemies in the period's heated philosophical and theological debates, and who later faced charges of heresy which made him flee for refuge to the Cluniac order. He was also an outstanding teacher, and the students who flocked to his lectures from all over Europe returned to their own countries with accounts of his renown.

Nor was Heloise's light under a bushel. Even before she and Abelard met she was celebrated in Paris for her abilities and extraordinary intelligence. This indeed was what made Abelard first aware of her, and when he found that she was beautiful too, he arranged to take lodgings in her uncle's house with the intention, as he himself tells us, of seducing her. But if Heloise's letters provide any indication of the immediate sequel, it was almost certainly Heloise who seduced Abelard.

But the chief reason for the couple's fame as lovers rests on their letters, which they began to exchange some fifteen years after the debacle of Abelard's castration. Abelard had written a long letter of consolation to a friend, seeking to put the friend's sufferings in a good light by contrasting them with his own woeful tale, which he therefore recounted, in effect giving his life story and a detailed account of his love affair with Heloise. Either he sent a copy of the letter to Heloise, or she came by it some other way; and she wrote to him, initiating the now celebrated correspondence.

The letters – more accurately, Heloise's letters – are exquisite. Full of passion and yearning, of undimmed erotic desire, of painful self-control, of the highest and most beautiful sentiment, they are almost unbearably poignant. Abelard's replies have a tendency to be stuffy and pompous, advising her to control her still-lively sexual impulses and to direct her energies to the service of God. Where her letters are instinct with warmth and longing, his are cold and sententious.

One truly wonders how it was possible for Abelard not to hurry to Heloise when he read her burning words:

You know, beloved, as the whole world knows, how much I have lost in you, how at one wretched stroke of fortune that supreme act of flagrant treachery robbed me of my very self in robbing me of you ... At every stage of my life up to now, as God knows, I have feared to offend you rather than God, and tried to please you more than him. It was your command, not love of God, which made me take the veil ... If Augustus himself, emperor of the whole world, thought fit to honour me with marriage and conferred all the earth on me for ever, it would be sweeter and more honourable to me to be, not his empress, but your whore.

These words were written, remember, after a decade and a half of silence between them.

The pleasures of lovers which we shared have been too sweet [she continues], they can never displease me, and can scarcely be banished from my thoughts ... Even during the celebration of the Mass, when our prayers should be purest, lewd visions of the pleasures we shared take such a hold on my unhappy soul that my thoughts are on their wantonness instead of on my prayers. Everything we did, and also the times and places, are stamped on my heart along with your image, so that I live through it all again with you.

The poignancy of these reminiscences is enhanced by the lucky discovery made by the scholar Constant Mews of portions of the lovers' letters written actually during the course of their affair, fragments tantalisingly incomplete but powerful nevertheless, and revealing not just of the scorching intensity of their love, but of the occasional quarrels and separations all too common a concomitant of high ardour.

Abelard does better in these early letters than in the later ones. With respect to the later part of the story history has been too kind to Abelard, given that it is Heloise who is the true heroine of the tale, her love and her honesty surviving intact while Abelard's post-testicular thoughts rose to lofty apologia, self-vindication and self-advertisement. Not that he needed to be self-advertising; he was after all the foremost logician and debater of the time, famous throughout Europe, feared by many in the Church establishment, and as it happens on the right side in the epoch's major philosophical dispute. (This was a quarrel over the question whether a 'universal' such as (say) whiteness exists independently of particular white things, as an abstract entity in which those particulars share, thus explaining why they are similar; or whether 'whiteness' is merely a word used by us to record our recognition of similarities. Espousers of the first view are called Realists, of the second Nominalists – and Abelard was the celebrated and redoubtable champion of the Nominalists.)

It is a charming and hopeful fact, however, that after the later correspondence started, a comradeship grew between the two, Abelard writing hymns for Heloise's convent, and occasionally visiting her there. It reminds us that even Darby and Joan swung from the chandeliers once, though not perhaps quite as vigorously, wonderfully and catastrophically as the philosopher and the brilliant and beautiful maiden who seduced him, like Thaïs in John Heath-Stubbs's 'Epitaph for Thaïs':

> Ask not how many young men their fortunes let slip,
>   and careers,
> Chancing one night on her couch (and it was worth it,
>   they said);
> Neo-platonic sages failed to show up at their lectures –
> Dream of the touch of her lips, metaphysics go hang!

Emerson
1803–1882

A few things divide American from British intellectual sensibility in addition (as Wilde observed) to the common language they are expressed in, and one of them is the scriptures
each tradition invokes – in the British case Carlyle, Ruskin,
Arnold, and in the American case Thoreau, Whitman, and the
man who influenced them both: Ralph Waldo Emerson.

After a sickly but long life Emerson died in 1882, thus
inhabiting most of the century which saw his country expand
from little more than his native New England to a continental
empire flooded by polyglot immigration. He was no mere
scholar – although 'scholar' was the title he chose to describe
himself, not as an academic but as the author of philosophical
poems and essays – for he was active in opposing slavery and the
expropriation of Native American lands in the great colonising
westward expansion that made today's United States. His reputation does not, however, rest on these commendable traits, far
ahead of their time as they were, but on his essays and the ideas
they contain.

'Nothing at last is sacred,' Emerson wrote, 'but the integrity
of your own mind.' This is a remarkably radical claim for his
time, and especially for a man descended from a long line of
Dissenting ministers, who had himself been licensed to preach –
in the Unitarian persuasion – by no less than the Harvard Div-
inity School. But Emerson quickly grew uneasy about the tenets
of revealed religion even as he preached them, and after just

three years in charge of a Boston congregation he found that he could no longer administer communion.

It was a Rubicon moment. He gave up his parish and travelled to Europe, where he met Coleridge, Wordsworth and Carlyle, establishing a friendship with the latter that lasted fifty years. While in Italy on this journey he also met Walter Savage Landor, and was told by the old poet, 'A man must slaughter his hundred oxen, whether or not he knows they will be eaten by gods or flies.' Oddly, despite the fact that Emerson would have missed this tremendous and inspiring utterance if he had not travelled, he later, upon settling for life near Concord, in Massachusetts, claimed that travel is a waste of time.

The ideas for which Emerson is most famous are 'transcendentalism', a mystic appreciation of the unity of all things, not least of man with nature; and 'self-reliance', by which he meant that people must free themselves from conventional ideas, and seek deep within themselves for the universal basis of the life best worth living. He intended self-reliance to be understood as a practice, a system of striving, which aimed at freeing the individual to conduct himself in a fully self-governed, clear-minded way. It is easy to see how both Thoreau and Whitman took inspiration from these thoughts, and worked them out – both in theory and practice – in their own lives.

The claim underlying Emerson's views about self-reliance is that each individual's fundamental self is a 'transpersonal universal'. He put the point by saying that 'the currents of the Universal Being circulate through me; I am part or particle of God'. Since 'God' is the oneness of all things, it follows that the individual is one with the universe. Most people do not realise this, Emerson claimed; they are stuck fast in conventional ways of seeing things. His chief desire was to free them from that illusion.

Although he resented the need to leave the privacy of his study in order to engage in public affairs, Emerson was never able to turn his back on the great questions of his day – and great they were. Abolition, socialism, emancipation of women, education, the fate of the 'Indians' being driven before the inexorable tide of expansion – all called upon his frail energies. Because he wrote so much he sometimes expressed himself in ways that appear at odds with the reforming spirit – seeming, for example, to spurn the poor ('Are they my poor?') in his famous essay 'Self Reliance'. But his version of moral socialism was genuine and deep-rooted, as evidenced by his life-long commitment to the cause of Abolition.

It is not very easy to read Emerson now. His style is often hyperbolic and over-decorated. His long, complex sentences are sometimes indistinguishable from the more prodigious efforts of the late Henry James, and the unsystematic, allusive, suggestive, insinuating way he advances his ideas – a tenebrous unfurling rather than a clear statement – offends the intellectual taste educated by the rigour and clarity of the best modern scholarship. But he repays reading; and although he is not alone among philosophers whose manner obscures their matter (or, too often, lack of it), there is indeed good matter in him to be gained from the effort.

Dostoevsky's *The Idiot*
1821–1881

To understand *The Idiot* it is best to look at how its themes emerged from Dostoevsky's preoccupations in the works he wrote during the four years beforehand. Between 1864 and 1868, writing under tremendous personal pressure, Dostoevsky produced three novels of philosophical fiction, at least two of them permanent classics of world literature. The first, written in 1864, is *Notes From Underground*. The second is *Crime and Punishment*, published in 1866. The third, completed in 1868, is *The Idiot*. They are not linked as a series, but by the unfolding of a theme; for they embody Dostoevsky's evolving attempt to understand and state the truth about ethics.

In the winter of 1863–4 Dostoevsky was ill, his wife was dying of tuberculosis, his mistress had betrayed him and gone to Paris, and in St Petersburg his stepson was wasting the money he struggled to send him. For nearly a year Dostoevsky had been unable to write. But then a commission from the *Epocha*, a new magazine, promised income, and at the same time he received a spur to his energies by reading Nikolai Gavrilovich Chernyshevsky's optimistically liberal *What Is To Be Done?*, which promoted the utopian ideal of a society in which free individuals attain happiness by satisfying their rational desires, under the sole constraint of not harming others. A follower of J. S. Mill, Chernyshevsky argued that the only true basis of morality is enlightened self-interest and reason; and correlatively, that evil is done only by those who do not understand their own best interests.

The *Notes From Underground* was an angry response to this view. 'I am a sick man. I am a malicious man. I am an unprepossessing man. I think I have a pain in my spleen.' So begins the novel, written straight from the anguish of Dostoevsky's circumstances yet far more than autobiography; for he wished to show that human beings are not fundamentally benign, as Chernyshevsky assumed, but are made of profoundly mixed metal. They might well know the difference between good and evil, yet they are capable of choosing the latter. 'Who was it, pray, who first declared that man behaves like a scoundrel only because he does not know his true interests ... O pure, innocent babe!' the *Notes* scornfully says.

This is the first statement of Dostoevsky's rejection of Enlightenment notions of rational morality in favour of the view that human psychology is irrational and chaotic. This view fed into one major strand of the modern European mind, as the direct ancestor of those modern movements in thought and art that premise pessimism and absurdity, and recognise – and sometimes even celebrate – the darkest aspects of human nature.

But Dostoevsky could not rest content with the negative implications of the *Notes*. He had an urgent desire to know whether it is possible to transcend conventional ideas of good and evil by choosing to act for reasons which, although conventionally describable as evil, would in fact represent an act of self-assertion or self-legislation in something like Nietzsche's sense, rather than the obedience that ordinary morality requires; a superman morality, chosen by the individual for himself in fulfilment of his superiority to the norm.

This is what Raskolnikov in *Crime and Punishment* tries to do. He decides to murder an old woman, and carries the decision out, later explaining his motivation in these terms: 'I wanted to kill without casuistry, to kill for my own sake ... it was not money I needed but something else ... I wanted to know, and to know quickly, whether I was a worm like everyone else, or a man. Shall I be able to transgress or shall I not? Shall I dare to stoop down and take, or not? Am I a trembling creature, or have I the *right*?'

Such was Raskolnikov's explanation for his act; but he was not so sure about its justification. He wavers between two alternatives, one the Nietzsche-like claim that because he is a superman he can make his own moral laws, the other a utilitarian one saying that because the victim was a hateful and hated old money-lender, her death benefited humanity.

But the essential point is that Raskolnikov finds he cannot live with what he has done; he becomes unnerved, feverish and strange; and eventually, in an agony of mind, he confesses. In Siberia after his trial he repents – not for having committed the murder, but either (and he is not quite sure which) for having been too weak to live with what he had done, or for having discovered that there is something in the human spirit that makes the attainment of 'moral superman' status impossible.

This dilemma is at the novel's heart. When he reached its end Dostoevsky suddenly saw that perhaps the story of the regeneration of a man like Raskolnikov could show how to resolve that dilemma. 'Here begins a new story,' the closing words of *Crime and Punishment* say, 'the story of the gradual renewal of a man, the story of his rebirth, of his gradual transition from one world to another, and of the revelation to him of a new, hitherto quite unknown reality.'

But Dostoevsky did not write the story of Raskolnikov's rebirth. Instead he went straight to the new reality, inhabited by a new and different kind of moral protagonist – a being of the sort a Raskolnikov could only become after an infinite journey across moral space. That being is the hero of *The Idiot*, Prince Myshkin, the 'positively good man', a holy fool, a saint-like figure, or even a Christ-like one (saying which is to forget the many disanalogies between a truly Myshkin-like character such as Chauncey Gardiner in Jerzy Kosinski's novel and film *Being There*, and Jesus-like characters who drive money-lenders from temples). Where Raskolnikov had made a febrile and failed effort at conquering morality, Myshkin succeeds; *The Idiot* is the story of a triumph, though of an utterly different order.

Dostoevsky had a clear conception of his aim in *The Idiot*. To his niece Sonya he wrote, 'The idea of the novel is my old favourite idea, but so difficult that for long I did not dare to try it; and if I try it now it is only because I am in a desperate situation. The principal aim of the novel is to depict the positively good man. There is nothing in the world more difficult ... it is an infinite task. The good is an ideal, and both our ideal and that of civilised Europe is far from being worked out. In the whole world there is only one positively good man, Christ.' In literature, Dostoevsky continued, there is Don Quixote and Pickwick; but they are good only because they are at the same time ridiculous. Both invite compassion because they are mocked by those far inferior to them in the worth they possess without knowing it. Victor Hugo's Jean Valjean is another example; but he provokes sympathy not for his undoubted goodness but for the injustice he suffers.

Apart from some explicit New Testament analogies and allusions (Myshkin gathers children round him; he is kind to a sinning woman; seeing an ass rouses him from his despondency), what seems most influential in shaping Dostoevsky's image of Myshkin is two striking figures. One is the *yurodivy*, the wandering beggar-pilgrim familiar in old Russia, whose physical and mental disabilities are signatures of holiness. Rogozhin indeed says to Myshkin, 'You are quite a yurodivy; and God loves such as you.'

The other is the Knight of the Sorrowful Countenance himself. He is by far the one who most readily comes to mind when seeking Myshkin's literary forebear. Dostoevsky wrote eloquently of 'the greatest and saddest book ever created by the genius of man' in *Journal of an Author*, and he has Aglaya quote

Pushkin's *Poor Knight* expressly in order to apply it to Myshkin. Though one takes the form of comedy and the other as tragedy, both *Don Quixote* and *The Idiot* are at bottom about the same thing: the conflict between reality and the ideal.

There is, though, a revealing difference between Quixote and Myshkin. Quixote seeks to express his goodness in action: he attacks the world's evils, he tilts at windmills. Myshkin is wholly passive. He is the embodiment of the renunciation and humility that one species of Christian view identifies as a supreme virtue, second only to faith. To achieve it requires humiliation and suffering, and Myshkin embraces both, without hesitation, at every opportunity. His morality is quintessentially that of the Beatitudes, where to mourn, to be poor, meek, reviled and persecuted, is to be blessed. This is a far cry from the Nietzschean self-assertion of Raskolnikov, and even further from Nietzsche's contempt for the 'slave morality' expressed by the Beatitudes, which in his view turn true morality upside down. Perhaps paradoxically, the examples of active goodness in *The Idiot* – Nastasya's self-sacrifice in refusing to marry Myshkin for his sake rather than her own, and Aglaya's uprightness and steadfastness, which are so much part of the charm of her innocence – are more attractive to the modern eye than Myshkin's negative energy. And yet his charisma is great: there is something breathtaking about his reply to the young man dying of tuberculosis and enraged at his fate, who asks Myshkin what he has to do to achieve an honourable death; and Myshkin quietly replies, 'Pass by us and forgive us our happiness.'

Of course there is no happiness at the end of Myshkin's foray home to Russia from his Swiss sanatorium. The novel ends with the horrific scene of the vigil kept by Myshkin and Rogozhin over Nastasya's murdered body: Rogozhin collapses with a brain-fever, and Myshkin returns to the idiocy from which the events of the novel have been only half an awakening, taking with him his simplicity, passivity, and unimpeachable goodness.

Is that goodness believable? Of course not: it is even a question whether someone who has no desires, feels no temptations, nor ever notices the smile on the face of seductive evil, can be called good. Writing of Tolstoy's Levin, when this latter had thrown aside Kant and the philosophers to adopt the simple faith of his peasants, Dostoevsky said, 'Two weeks after the end of the novel Levin will snag his soul on a rusty nail.' Levin was a promissory note; Tolstoy later explored more fully the idea of a real person aspiring (with few guarantees of success) to be a 'positively good man', in the figure of Prince Nekhlyudov in *Resurrection*. But it is Dostoevsky who tried the more ambitious experiment of placing a holy fool in a world of passions and desires, and allowing the strange logic of the situation to pursue itself home. As a result *The Idiot* is one of the most excoriating, compelling and remarkable books ever written; and without question one of the greatest.

Jung
1875–1961

Only to their diminishing numbers of *aficionados* do Freud and Jung have more than curiosity value now, a century after the first impulse was given to the pseudo-scientific psychological theories and associated therapies associated with their names. Freud looms largest on that rearward horizon, perhaps because his theories are more focused, are rooted in the ever-intriguing matter of sex, and come packaged in compelling narratives of strange human experiences – for Freud was a remarkably skilful writer. Jung's more diffuse and unwieldy theories did not have quite the same potency, but both men managed to capture the imagination of a reeling humanity in the bloody and disastrous first half of the twentieth century.

Whereas Freud concentrated upon the individual mind, Jung believed that every mind contains far more than experience alone can give it, acquired from a shared transpersonal source he called 'the collective unconscious', a deep pool of beliefs, ideas and attitudes shaped by the formative experiences of mankind from earliest history, and containing 'archetypes' which are in effect mythic idealisations (the Hero, the Mother) constituting innate forms that shape human experience. These archetypes manifest themselves in consciousness as symbols, and dreams provide an especially rich access to them. That is the reason why Jung spent so much time examining mythologies, primitive religions, alchemy, the occult, flying saucers and dreams in pursuit of an inclusive account of humanity's submerged mental stock. The key to his view is that mental problems arise when the individual psyche is out of step with the collective unconscious. Jungian therapy consists in reconciling the two.

Jung was a Swiss Protestant who qualified as a doctor, specialised in psychiatry, married a wealthy woman, and took at the flood the early twentieth century's anxious fascination with the unconscious mind. Like the other giants of emerging psychotherapy he was therefore a Savonarola of his time, and disciples – mainly women – flocked to him. Being a man as well as a guru, he took advantage of that fact in the predictable way, among other things incorporating his main mistress into his household, and regularly taking both her and his wife with him when he travelled.

Jung's being Swiss and Protestant meant that in the 1930s he was a useful figurehead for the increasingly Nazi-dominated psychological society, run from Berlin, which served as the international centre for studies in the field. Even tacit or reluctant collaboration with Nazism does no one from that period any good, and Jung's reputation has suffered badly therefore. But although his own theories made him talk about 'national character' (and thus to generalise about Jews and to distinguish them from Germans) in ways that the Nazis found useful to quote, he also made efforts to help Jewish victims of Nazism. These contradictions and ambiguities were typical of him.

Jung lived a long time – 1875 to 1961 – in a tumultuous period, and did and wrote much, so any complete account of him has to be long. But history is sometimes cruelly just in its summary judgements, and the emerged consensus on Jung's work, bluntly stated, is that it is vitiated by its eclectic baggage of mysticism, superficial anthropology, credulity and superstition. Freud, at least, was an empiricist and rationalist, which explains his eventual disdain for Jung's excesses; and even Freud is thought by many now to be off (scientifically speaking) with the fairies.

Bernard Williams
1929–2003

British philosophy since the beginning of the twentieth century has been a strange affair, at least to lay eyes. Abstruse, remote and technical, it has appeared to distance itself from the practical affairs of the world, reprising the era of the medieval Schoolmen by losing itself in dense fogs of jargon devised to capture the last possible refinement of distinction-drawing and abstraction.

Success as a philosopher in this professionalised version of the enterprise has required not just high intelligence and rigorous academic training, but a special cast of intellect, consisting in power, style, finesse, subtlety and depth. The four outstanding figures in British academic philosophy during the last half-century have been exemplars of these characteristics, and each most especially of one: Michael Dummett for power, P. F. Strawson for style, David Wiggins for finesse, Bernard Williams for subtlety – and all for depth.

With the exception of Strawson, these doyens show that contemporary philosophers are not so remote from ordinary concerns after all. Wiggins once campaigned on transport in London. Dummett gave many years to the struggle against racism. Williams was a distinguished chairman of a government commission on pornography, advised a Labour government, and kept faith with his centre-left commitments.

True, these public engagements do not seem to flow directly from these thinkers' technical work – except in the case of

Williams. Nor have they been easy and regular voices in the public media – except in the case of Williams. Nor have these thinkers strayed far from Oxford – except in the case of Williams, who held distinguished professorships on both sides of the Atlantic. Williams, in short, was more expansive than his fellow Parnassians in geographical and public respects, which is why he was more salient in the national consciousness.

His last book, *Truth and Truthfulness*, captured themes that were always central to his philosophical work. Most of that work concerned ethics. It was not exclusively so; he wrote a brilliant study of Descartes, and contributed greatly to the debate about personal identity which has exercised philosophers since John Locke identified it as a problem. But although discussion of neither of these subjects is complete without reference to Williams, his rich, searching and complex contributions to ethics are his best work.

Two messages ring out from it. One is that moral values are a function of circumstances. There are no independent, objective values as there are independent, objective scientific facts. Instead, what we should care about, and how we should live, depends on how we feel and what we seek in the social and historical situation we find ourselves in. Values are a function of emotions and desires, and luck has a large part to play in shaping both by setting the parameters within which they fluctuate.

The second message is that ethics is not a matter for moral philosophy alone. History, the sciences, sociology and politics all bear on how things are with people, and how therefore they do or should to choose to live.

The connection between the two messages is obvious. Equally obvious is what they meant for Williams's attitude to the major ethical theories of the past, particularly utilitarianism – which enjoins maximising benefit for the greatest number – and Kantian theory, which says that ethics is fundamentally about duty. Williams was hostile to both kinds of view, and not just because they share the idea that ethics has objective foundations. He rejected utilitarianism because he did not think questions of value can be reduced to a single metric of benefits, and because it impugns individual integrity – for example, by requiring one to do wrong when the calculation of benefits says that doing so will maximise them elsewhere.

One reason Williams rejected Kantian ethics is that the motive it offers for action is an agent's recognition of an abstract rational demand. For Williams, only a desire felt by the agent himself can count as a genuine reason for action. He echoed David Hume in saying that the fact that something follows from a rationally-apprehended principle cannot by itself motivate an agent; only the agent's own wishes can stir him into getting up and acting one way or another.

Williams held that our beliefs about what is valuable in the moral sense are many and inconsistent. There are similarities between this view and Isaiah Berlin's thesis that society embraces a plurality of mutually unresolvable values and interests. But Williams was uncompromising about what that means: in the moral life, he said, there are only points of view.

But this does not mean that ethical practice is an arbitrary or, worse, a pointless thing. In *Ethics and the Limits of Philosophy* Williams argued that our ethical practice should be able to stand up to reflection, using 'reflective social knowledge', including history, to make a critique of our ethics possible. Subjecting our ethical practice to reflective critique amounts to 'truthfulness', while the availability of the required social knowledge means that we have access to forms of truth in the ethical realm, even if it is not the ideal objective truth of science. And truth and truthfulness thus understood together make sense of the idea, Williams said, that there can be meaningful individual lives, lived in society with others and sharing those others' perceptions 'to a considerable depth'.

These ideas occur at the end of *Ethics and the Limits of Philosophy* as a kind of promissory note, expressive of the hope that is left even when one grasps, as Williams wished us to grasp, his two uncompromising messages about ethics. In his last book the ideas of truth and truthfulness received full-length treatment. Instead of linking them directly to the project left implicit in the earlier work, Williams remotivated discussion of them by pointing to an apparent tension between our desire for truthfulness (at least in the form of suspicion, an intention not to be misled or fooled) and a disbelief in, or at least doubt about, whether there is indeed such a thing as truth. The two points, and the fact that they are not inconsistent, are highly consequential – not just for ethics, but for politics and all intellectual endeavours outside the hard sciences.

From a rich blend of resources Williams constructed a case for defending both truth and truthfulness as intellectual and practical values. Part of his case is made by telling a story about how truth came to matter, part is made by showing what would be lost if the fashion for disbelieving in the possibility of truth were to take root. In the process he identified two fundamental concepts in the notion of truth, Accuracy and Sincerity, the first a requisite of the search for truth, and the second a requisite in reporting it.

In the process of exploring these ideas Williams took a journey through a number of closely related debates, about authenticity, liberty, relativism, and the narratives we use to make sense of things. His original two messages remained unchanged; we are still in the grey regions without hard ethical principles, where individual lives have to be negotiated in the midst of their circumstances. This is a picture complicated further by Williams's demonstration that even such notions as sincerity have changed their content in time. But at least the values of truthfulness and truth are handholds in the uncertain light, which gives hope, Williams claimed, that lives and institutions that depend on the virtues of truth will 'keep going'.

Williams aimed to preserve notions of truth and truthfulness while conceding everything implied by his two messages. Did he succeed? To do so his writings must persuade us that there cannot be objective truth in morality; that the plurality of situations which alone, in his view, give content to ethical judgements are not a mere mask for personal preferences; that it is true – something the Stoics long ago denied – that luck is an ineliminable feature of the moral life; that philosophy's pretensions to identify the good independently of contingent circumstances are genuinely empty. And he must persuade us that the only true reasons for moral action are individual desires.

These are all large and interesting matters, and Williams discussed them and the rest of his ethical views with eloquence and subtlety. There is something bleak about his outlook, yet hopeful too; for it shows that notions treasured in traditional ethics, such as truth and truthfulness themselves, retain a central place in the barer landscape he describes.

Perhaps that is why Williams chimed with our times, because in the failure of faiths to reassure us, in the loss of old certainties providing moral anchorage, and in the irrelevance and directionlessness of much intellectual endeavour, a sceptical but reflective view such as his gives hope that a workable way of living for the good can still be found.

Edward Said
1935–2003

E dward Said was a much-interviewed man, partly because he stood in a unique cross-cultural place at a painful historical juncture, and could speak about it with intelligence and eloquence, thus attracting the persistent attention of journalists and fellow intellectuals; and partly because he agreed so often to be interviewed, doubtless out of the intellectual's need for expression, but almost certainly also because there was more than a tincture of vanity in that handsome man who derived so much from so many places – Palestine, the Western literary tradition, the East, America, the British public-school tradition, the Arab world, the East Coast Ivy League tradition, Cairo, Jerusalem, New York, Beirut, well-lit European television studios, the border with Israel at whose fence he threw stones – because he could claim to belong to none of them though benefiting massively from them all.

The many interviews he gave between them beautifully manifest these paradoxical self-positionings and deep ambiguities, and in the process offer a portrait – all the more striking for being so unselfconsciously self-conscious – of a vitally interesting individual. A volume collecting his interviews was ready for publication shortly before his lamented death, and he therefore read it; one wonders whether he saw how chameleon-like he was, taking on the colours of the side from which his interviewers came: an Arab for Arabs, a 'colonial' when talking to other 'colonials' (e.g. the Indian editor of the volume), and a

culturally conservative four-square Western-educated intellectual for Western academic colleagues. He even went so far
as to say to Israel's *Ha'aretz* magazine, 'I'm the last Jewish
intellectual ... I'm a Jewish-Palestinian.'

He was, of course, nothing of the sort, and not much of
the other things either. Born a Protestant Christian in West
Jerusalem of wealthy Christian Arab parents, he spent his early
life in Cairo being educated at a famous English public school
there along with the later King Hussein of Jordan and the actor
Omar Sharif, and then went to university in America. After
taking his PhD in English Literature he joined the faculty of
Columbia University in the early 1960s, and New York
remained his home until his death.

But although his chosen milieu was American academia, the
accident of his origins gave him a stake in the tragedy of the
Middle East, and he became an indefatigable and powerful advo-
cate of the Palestinian cause. Fame came with his book *Orientalism*, whose argument is that Europeans dealt with the Orient
through a process of colonisation premised on the Orient as
'Other' and expressed in many ways, from literature and art
to scholarship and thence colonial bureaucracy. He saw the
Occident–Orient relationship as deriving not in fact from alien-
ation but from historical closeness, although at its fullest it
takes the form of power, dominance, and varying degrees of
hegemony in Gramsci's sense of 'cultural domination'. This
important idea, and its extension into Said's views about the
relation of culture and imperialism generally, is discussed
repeatedly and from a variety of angles in the interviews he
gave, which between them therefore constitute a work in itself,
and an excellent introduction to his thought.

For all that Said was a campaigner for Palestine and an enemy
of Zionism in unequivocal terms (he disliked Martin Luther
King because King was pro-Israel), he was otherwise a small-c
conservative in cultural terms. Despite everything he said about
Orientalism, his most abiding loyalty was to Western High

Culture (he loved serious music and opera, and wrote about it frequently) and the literature of the English tongue. Claiming that even Jane Austen embodies the imperialising thrust of English literature – Mansfield Park is paid for by a slave plantation in Antigua, a passingly mentioned item which for Said, as for the many engaged in the industry of 'postcolonial literary studies', is an endless resource – Said was able to be a prophet among the avant-garde lit.-crit. fraternity, and yet at the same time he early came to despise them. Refreshingly, he was sometimes dismissive of 'literary theory' and the jargon-laden 'auto-tinkering' of the academy, in which literary criticism is a cheap form of philosophy done by waving banners with 'Derrida' and 'Heidegger' on them, resulting in salaried logorrhoea, a thick stream of indecipherable nonsense that has spewed, like outfall from a mains sewer, into an intellectually polluted sea of futility.

But interviews with him show that he never quite escaped the grip of this intellectual disease. When speaking to fellow lit.-crit. academics he falls easily into the jargon: 'As Foucault said ... As Derrida said ...' is the familiar refrain, and like his colleagues he typically misquotes and misrepresents (as when he shows unfamiliarity with what e.g. Hobbes and Popper really meant, though airily invoking their names in that lit.-crit. way, which is like a verbal tic or twitch: '... as Popper said...').

As just one of many ambiguities that cluster round Said's intellectual persona, though, his divided attitude to his academic discipline is understandable enough. Often pressed in interviews on the question of how he can regard Austen and Conrad as great writers, and their works as great literature, while at the same time viewing them as imperialist producers of texts not merely expressing but embodying the very process of colonisation and therefore diminishment of the Other, Said had to navigate carefully between emphasising now one side of the dilemma and now the other, trying to show that a work can be great literature even if it is, because it is of its time and place, an instrument of a form of harm. To perceptions which catch less shiftingly grey nuances, this seems like having a cake and eating it; much of what Said tried to do in interviews was to show how that can be done.

One thing that everyone can agree with Said about – and it is a point he often and eloquently made – is that the academy should not be disengaged from the real world and especially the injustices it contains. His own life is a monument to that conviction, and deserves praise for it.

Ideas

Art, Society and Civilisation

Think of 'civilisation' as denoting not a thing but a process: the process of civilising people and the practices and institutions which, because human beings are essentially social creatures, they create (whether consciously or by process of historical accretion) to make living together possible. Merely to glance at a fully mature civil society is to see immediately the elaborate structures which create and sustain it, from government and a system of laws to the manners and customs which lubricate transactions between individuals, groups, genders and generations – the civic etiquette, you might say – binding society together at its base. Many tributaries feed into the mighty stream of what makes civil society thus possible, from education and tradition to enforcement by the society's institutional agencies. But one of the chief of them, in particular connection with the 'civil' part of the equation, is the arts.

The connection between the arts and civilisation is at once obvious and immensely complicated. An empirically supported guess is that the ancestors of the arts (wall painting, body decorating, singing and dancing) arose in relation to the religious beliefs and practices which formed social bonds in the earliest human communities, and were therefore central from the outset. This binding function was undoubtedly soon joined by a progressive function, arising from the way the arts challenge and re-interpret; for it is likely that the playful, creative, entertainment-seeking and sense-making qualities that distinguish the human mind would quickly see the recreational and philosophical potential in these activities, so apt are they for both.

However it happened, once the genie of arts escaped its lamp, its power to challenge as well as bind must have been quickly apparent, for throughout recorded history the arts have prompted ambiguous reactions: they have been suborned to social needs on the one hand, and subjected to censorship and control on the other. The former is a mark of their civilising role, the latter of how the process of civilisation cannot be reduced to the maintenance of orthodoxies. Pindar celebrated the great champions of the Games, immortalising the qualities of grace, skill and prowess which Greek antiquity placed at the heart of its moral striving. Plato said that he would ban poetry because fiction is a form of lying, and anyway traduced the gods (he had in mind such matters as Homer's account of the adultery of Aphrodite with Ares, the source of the 'Homeric laughter' of the gods). Popes and Florentine nobles commissioned paintings and sculptures; American Congressmen threaten to withhold public funding for the arts when outraged by such productions as Andres Serrano's *Piss Christ*. The same underlying sentiments are at work on both sides of these cases, across a span of two and a half millennia, marvellously illustrating the human need for art and art's more than human power to disturb.

But the binding and challenging aspects of art's power are not merely not inconsistent, they both play the civilising role under discussion. When the arts bind, they constitute an expression of identity, a record of communal experience, a celebration of values and things valued. When they challenge, they vent criticism, release frustrations, signal aspirations, and offer alternatives. In both cases they are fundamental voices in the debate society has with itself at the public level, just as, at the personal level, they are fundamental voices in the dialogue responsive individuals have with themselves, and the people in their immediate circle, about life and how to live it. In particular, they do this by expanding the possibilities for insight into our own and other dispensations. 'Thanks to art,' said Proust, 'instead of seeing one world, our own, we see it multiplied, and as many original artists as there are, so many worlds are at our disposal.'

If these claims seem too large, as they assuredly will to those many who think that the arts have always been an avocation for the relatively few (generally for those privileged enough to have the leisure to enjoy them), then it becomes important to note that the phrase so far used – 'the arts' – embraces a continuum whose one end is often hard to differentiate from the entertainments of demotic culture (television soap operas, romantic novels, films, pop songs) and whose other end consists in such familiar high-culture staples as opera, literature, Renaissance painting and classical music. There is no single definition of what makes an activity fall under the label 'the arts'; rather, they share what Wittgenstein called a family resemblance. Matters are complicated by the ultra-capacious view now current, nicely summed up in Andy Warhol's definition of art as 'what you can get away with', which includes a variety of activities and objects which once would have come nowhere near wearing the label. Of course, the fact that the boundaries of demotic culture and art blur at one end of the spectrum does not mean that there is no distinction between them: negotiating it there is merely harder; but the task of discernment, of taste, and of having and applying standards and good judgement, remains necessary.

But to see how the arts play their civilising role, both as contributing cohesion and as challenging ossifications, it is worth reminding ourselves of the two clearest cases: drama and the novel. With them in view it is easier to see how some of the other arts – say, painting – work in closely allied ways.

A single illustration can do all the work of illumination here. Take a very familiar example: Austen's *Pride and Prejudice*. Among the things this novel does is explore a central aspect of interpersonal relationships: the mutual evaluation of character that makes relationships possible. Elizabeth Bennet and Darcy misread one another at the outset, and on Elizabeth's part the misunderstandings feed on the application of Darcy's beliefs about social status and its obligations, for he deliberately blights the matrimonial chances of Elizabeth's sister, believing (on grounds legitimate in the Austenian world-view) that the Bennets are 'inferior' to himself and his circle, given the deplorable failings in most respects of Elizabeth's mother. What he learns quite quickly is that personal merit outweighs considerations of class, and what she learns eventually is that there is a form of pride, as an emotion of self-assessment, which attaches legitimately to certain responsibilities of inheritance and family – a view Austen would have expected the readers of her own day to share and admire, although we now might not.

This is only one thread, though a major one, in *Pride and Prejudice*, but its effect on reflective readers is to invite them to reconsider the question of the bases on which people evaluate each other in forming relationships. Anyone who learned something from this exploration would have thereby been offered an opportunity to profit. He might not take it; it might have a negative effect. There are no guarantees about what effect, if any, a work of art will have, whether or not intended by its creator. The point is that it opens a space where an opportunity for profit arises, whichever side of the argument a thoughtful reader comes down on.

This is not for a moment to suggest that art has moral responsibilities. That way lies censorship, the worst fate both for art and for the civilisation it helps produce. Responsive consumption of works of art is neither necessary nor sufficient for anyone to form and pursue any recognisable conception of the good; but there is more possibility that it might than if no one cared, and humankind were abandoned to what a world without the arts would most have to offer: ignorance, parochialism and crudity.

Drama is not more explicitly didactic than the novel, it only appears so. Fielding, Dickens, George Eliot and Gissing are as eager to address moral perplexities and social injustices as, in their avowed ways, are Wilde and Shaw. But it does not take Harold Bloom to remind us that merely by capturing the variety of human motive and sensibility, Shakespeare provides wall-to-wall mirrors reflecting the human condition, and in ways that drive home its possibilities, whether of anguish, beauty or hope. Just to see the moral and psychological range displayed – say, from Iago to Othello, from Desdemona to Cassio – is to learn something valuable.

The extension to other arts can rapidly be established. Again examples suffice. When Renaissance painters extended themselves beyond the industrial production of religious images into secular portraits, mythological allegories capturing the psychological insights of their originals, landscapes and still lifes celebrating the beauties of nature and its fruits, they were not abandoning the Gothic work of iterating the community's central values and aspirations, and its metaphysical portrait of heaven, hell and the fate of souls. Rather, they were redirecting attention away from exclusive focus on the transcendent and back to the immanent, to the world of people and their quotidian joys and desires. That was just as much a discussion of what matters to human experience as anything that had gone before, or would later come through other media of expression; in fact, true to human inventiveness, it was just another step in the power of doing so.

Almost everyone likes to be entertained, distracted, amused, surprised and pleased, whether by a juggler or a film, by bright lights and colours. Not everything that entertains and pleases – not every case of bright lights and colours – is art, if 'art' has a status differentiated by criteria of quality. Art entertains and amuses, and sometimes definitely intends to do no more; sometimes it has no intention other than just to exist, saying nothing and offering nothing so far, at least, as its maker's wishes go. All this has to be acknowledged. But most of the time the mere impact of an art work is enough to give it, among its entertaining, amusing, etc., effects, that consequence of making a consumer of it pause; and in those pauses, taken in sum, lie some of the main foundations of civilisation.

A sceptic might argue against this thesis by saying that the arts are consumed by minorities, and usually those with the means and the time for them – people, in other words, not in need of what art can be supposed to offer. This is true, but it is not quite the truth the sceptic thinks it is. As populations increase, so do the numbers in their reading, theatre-going, exhibition-visiting minorities. More people than ever before in history, in absolute terms, now enjoy the arts. In any big city exhibitions are crowded and concerts fully booked, markers not just of the status enjoyed by the arts, but by the related fact that appreciation of them is a self-encouraging phenomenon: the more people come to enjoy them, the more they wish to enjoy them. 'Art comes to you proposing frankly to give nothing but the highest quality to your moments as they pass,' said Walter Pater; that is a lesson which, once learned, is hard to forget.

A point that, in this connection, bears constant iteration is that when a reflective and responsive mind engages with the arts, it is nourished by them, and learns something immensely valuable from them, namely how to be discerning. 'It is only the dullness of the eye that makes any two things seem alike,' Pater also said. A realisation of the uniqueness and particularity of things carries over from a story, a painting or musical performance to a moral circumstance or an encounter with another human individual. In this way art civilises, because it is, as Shaw says, the mirror for souls.

Where does the artist himself or herself figure in this? Pliny the Elder tells us, in the last book of his celebrated *Natural History*, that Apelles, the most famous painter of antiquity, was paid 'the wealth of a small town' for each painting he produced. *Plus ça change*! One of Apelles' sayings has become a proverb: *'Nulla dies sine linea'* ('Never a day without a line'). When asked why he was a greater painter than his rivals he said, 'It is because I know when to lift my hand' – that is, when to stop.

Despite the esteem in which craftsmen, architects, sculptors and painters have almost always been held, many acquiring great wealth and status, it is only recently that the (so to say) 'artsiness' of artists has existed. The great painters of the Renaissance saw themselves as craftsmen or technicians; they had assistants who worked closely with them, painting much of each canvas commissioned by churches, palaces, guilds and private patrons, for all of whom a standard repertoire of subjects, from religious themes, portraits and attractive nudes to allegories and hunting scenes, had a standard range of formats which the patron expected to see in the completed work.

It is with the Romantic movement that the self-conscious 'artist' appeared. In antiquity it was believed that artistic creativity was not the spontaneous work of an individual, but the result of divine inspiration ('in-spir-ation' – literally, 'breathing in'). You saw your neighbour tending his olive trees next door, and wondered how on earth he – a mere man, a mere mortal – had managed to write (say) the *Iliad*. Answer: the Muses had breathed it, into him; he was a conduit for their creations, their messenger. 'Genius' meant 'a spirit', a benign demon, who sat on the messenger's shoulder and whispered in his ear. The Romantics internalised the concept of genius; 'I myself AM the genius,' they said. The more they laboured over their work, revising and improving it, the more it became their own. They were thus the originators, the creators, not merely messengers of the gods.

It then became a mark of honour to 'be an artist' – to starve in a garret, to have a wild eye 'in a fine frenzy rolling', lean cheeks and a Byronic lock falling over one eyebrow; to suffer for art, to burn with inner imperatives, as if scorched by the treasure destined to benefit mankind – if not contemporary mankind (since they will not buy), then a more intelligent posterity.

The wonderful facility of some artists does make it seem as

though gods worked in them. Stories abound about Mozart's easy genius, producing concerti and operas like rabbits from a hat as he hurried in his coach from one engagement to another. One tale tells of an anxious impresario banging on Mozart's door demanding a symphony he had commissioned, which was scheduled for rehearsal the very next day. Mozart put his head out of an upstairs window and called, 'I've finished it!' 'Thank God!' the impresario called back in relief, 'Give it to me!' to which Mozart replied, 'One moment: I just have to write it down.' Yet studies of the original manuscripts of the six string quartets composed by Mozart in honour of his beloved Hayden (K421, K465) show that he often worked at great length, with much revision and afterthought. For all that he was an artist in every sense of the word, he was a craftsman too.

Critics of contemporary art or 'art' see much of what is done today as standing in sharp contrast to work of the quality, depth and creative power associated with the likes of Mozart. When Ivan Massow quitted the Institute of Contemporary Arts in London he famously described much of what passes for contemporary art as 'pretentious, self-indulgent, craftless tat'. One response is to say that even if he is right, which he certainly is, it does not matter, for two reasons. One rests on the principle that it takes a lot of compost to grow a flower, so one should expect a high volume of 'tat' for each work of genuine merit. The second is that most of what will in time come to count as the best of the present day's art might not yet be even recognised as such by its contemporaries – in discussing this point elsewhere I cited web-page designs, certain films, photographs, and television works, certain cars and planes, certain presently unsung paintings (for painting will never cease to be important despite the fact that it is scarcely taught in art schools any longer) and doubtless other things that presently do not even occur to us.

The controversy, uncertainty and ambiguity which surround contemporary debates about art and 'art' in great part lies with

the sharp disjunction between the art market and what is produced by the people coming out of today's art schools. People
who buy art generally wish to buy pictures and sculptures; art
school graduates produce videos, installations, performances,
'conceptual art'. Not many potential art purchasers have the
room for large structures of scrap iron welded together, however
conceptually commendable; and those who do are unlikely to
want to. Of course artists must produce what their inner prompting tells them to, and some of them – if they are good of
their kind – will re-educate the public accordingly. But when
potential buyers see beauty, skill, interest, colour, form, striking comment on the world or human experience, a window
into other places of reality or imagination, added value
(psychologically, aesthetically) to their habitual environment –
remembering that most people who buy art like to display it in
their homes or places of work, and therefore plan to live with
it – the lack of fit becomes a matter for discussion. Most contemporary would-be art is ephemeral, or at any rate does not
bear repetition (who apart from a real enthusiast would have a
video running continuously for years in his home?) And that is
a pivotal thought; for if there is one thing art most often is, it is
something that retains its hold.

The value of what offers itself as art has several sources, some
in aspects of the work itself and some in its reception. A good
illustration is afforded by what is arguably the present day's
most cutting-edge art form: contemporary dance. A formidably
high level of basic skill is required before anything can be built
upon it; there is no pretending about the elements, and just
about everyone who watches another person dance can tell
the difference between the skilled and trained dancer and the
leaden-footed incompetent. From the outset, therefore, there
are criteria. Add to this ineliminable basis some imaginative
and striking choreography, and you have the reason why dance
so unequivocally counts as art even in this equivocal age.

Most of the present's other putative art forms, by contrast, rest on little but the claims of the self-appointed artist. Much of it strains after novelty or shock value instead of excellence in its kind, a notion which in any case probably seems quaint to most practitioners. It is scarcely surprising that such work fails to command any form of consensus among interested observers.

But this just invites iteration of the point about 'compost', needed so that the good can grow. So matters are as they should be; and in this mature state both of civilisation and the arts, the possibility for forming good judgements of the really worthwhile is more than ever alive. That fact itself shows how the arts have civilised society: where there is no such thing as a debate about the standards of dance and painting, musical and theatrical performance, literary and architectural quality, there is certainly no civilisation.

Allergies and the Zeitgeist

A forgotten fact about the Renaissance is that its denizens, for all their sophistication otherwise, were mortally afraid of being murdered. They mainly feared being poisoned by 'aqua tofana', an odourless, colourless toxin indistinguishable from ordinary drinking water, which could be slipped unnoticed into food or drink and which would incrementally kill its consumers. It was reputedly the weapon of choice for Lucrezia Borgia, the epoch's favourite bogeywoman. But there was, in fact, no such thing as aqua tofana; its existence is what we now call an 'urban myth'. Lucrezia, who deserved her reputation, had her victims stabbed and strangled as often as she poisoned them; and when she poisoned them it was with arsenic or henbane.

This Renaissance scare reprised a widespread fear of poisons at the height of the Roman Empire a thousand years earlier, and for the same reasons. Prior to Rome's epoch of imperial luxury, austerer Republican virtues of stoicism and endurance, prompted by the existence of real enemies on wild frontiers, prevented too much self-coddling. At the height of the Pax Romana the human need for something to fear – a need which is a survival instinct, as rooted in humans as in all other creatures – reasserted itself, and might have focused on real diseases if Rome had not had a clean water supply, excellent sewers, and an absence of motorised transport, thereby obliging people to walk. They were healthy and safe; so the vacuum came to be filled by imaginary dangers.

Exactly the same is happening now in the rich West, with 'allergy' as the high-tech substitute for 'poison', serving the same role as a hidden danger to well-being. Yet allergies are only a hundred years old – or at least, the name is. It was coined by Austrian paediatrician Clemens Pirquet to describe reactions suffered by children who had been given horse serum to combat infection. At first Pirquet used the term to denote any response, benign or otherwise, of the immune system to a foreign substance: *allos* is ancient Greek for 'different', and *ergos* means 'work'. But it quickly came to mean a bad reaction, and ever since then allergies, real and imagined, have never ceased multiplying in number.

Some of them are of course genuine, and some of the increases are worrying, especially the doubling of asthma cases in the developed world over the last twenty years. Some allergies which now take severe forms have long existed in milder guise; hay fever, dust-mite allergy, and the skin's response to irritants like nettles and flea-bites.

But many of the other supposed allergies acquired by rich Western humanity since Pirquet's time are doubtful entities. It seems that 50 million Americans claim to be allergic to something or other – that is one in five of the population – and between them they spend 10 billion dollars annually on remedies. Such figures immediately prompt sceptics to think, 'Hmm: cherchez la pharmaceutical company.' It is not unknown for medicine-makers to find the medicine before inventing the disease it cures or (better, since cure is bad for business) controls.

Moreover, many cases of bad *allos ergos* are caused by medical practices themselves. In America every year a hundred thousand people die, and a million more are harmed, as a direct result of medical treatment.

Drug companies are not however the real culprits. They are, after all, only responding to a climate of belief to the effect that the physical world out there is a potentially hostile, toxic place – that irritants and pathogens, pollutants and parasites, processed foods and chemical additives, are surreptitiously but steadily eroding health and well-being. Health and well-being are now regarded as the right of everyone with a bank account, and any derogation from the expected sunny norm has to be blamed on something. The candidates have become legion: the gluten in wheat, the fumes from traffic, the mysterious emanations from electricity pylons and communications masts.

But the truth is that we live in an era which has never been healthier and safer for people in the West, despite the existence of terrorism. This prompts our need for a new focus of anxiety. In places where major terrorist atrocities have occurred there has reportedly been a (temporary) drop in 'healthy living' practices and more alcohol and tobacco consumption, a fact foolishly celebrated by pro-smoking organisations. The point nicely illustrates the difference between how we respond to real external threats and (mainly) imaginary internal ones.

Paradoxically, we are also better informed about health, and know in general terms what is good for us. But this has a downside: we have become prone to health scares, to blaming 'allergens' for failures and unhappiness, to seeking medical solutions to life's problems. We are less tolerant of low-level aches and pains. We eat too much and exercise too little, and take pills to ease both the heartburn and the heartache that ensue. What we are mainly allergic to, in fact, is the lack of real threats to our well-being – apart from the self-inflicted ones of laziness, excess and stress. This is not to underestimate the real suffering of those whom pollutants genuinely poison, or of children gasping for breath in our smog-ridden cities. But it reminds us that our imaginations can be the most poisonous of all substances.

White-Collar Boxing

L ately, it seems, successful City professionals have found a new way of discharging the tensions of corporate life: by exchanging their pinstripes for boxing gloves and going three rounds with each other at the gym. Bemused observers might wonder what this says about the spirit of the age. Have people come to feel so insulated from reality by large bank balances and deep-pile carpets that they have to remind themselves of it by hitting each other?

'White-collar boxing' is not, however, new. Although regarded as the resource of poor boys seeking a quick exit from the slums, boxing has always principally been an upper-class sport, and not just for spectating. In the early nineteenth century young aristocrats flocked to 'Gentleman' Jackson's gym in London's Tottenham Court Road, Lord Byron among them, to learn the pugilistic art, and in doing so they were conscious of its ancient lineage, for at school they had read Homer's account of how Epeus (later builder of the Wooden Horse) beat Euryalus at the funeral games for Patroclus, and in Virgil's *Aeneid* how the gigantic but aged Entellus accepted the challenge of Dares by throwing his 'blood-and brain-bespattered' cestus into the ring.

Pugilism (which is bare fisted unlike boxing which requires padded gloves) was popular with well-born Athenian youths, who paid high fees to learn it. It returned to aristocratic fashion in the eighteenth century, both as recreation and as a spectator sport. Prize fights, which went on until one contestant could no longer stand, commanded huge purses and immense bets. Hazlitt famously wrote about one such in an essay regarded by

Gene Tunney, world heavyweight champion and editor of a boxing anthology, as the best fight description ever written.

As the distinction between pugilism and boxing suggests, the latter is a recent sport. In the ancient world pugilists sometimes wrapped their hands in leather thongs – in Rome they added lead weights and spikes for extra effect – which shows that the thongs were the contrary of protective devices. Padded gloves were used for practice in antiquity, but it was only with the introduction of the Queensberry Rules in 1866 that they became standard for amateur contests, and soon after for professional ones, thus creating boxing proper.

London's 'white-collar' boxers might know their Byron and Homer, but the proximate source of their hobby is doubtless America's 'Toughman' craze, in which untrained amateurs fight one another for a purse, or try to defeat a trained boxer who challenges all comers. If the dangers of recreational boxing needed highlighting, the 'Toughman' experience will oblige; it is now banned in ten US states because, since its inception in 1979, it has seen twelve deaths.

And this points a moral. In other dangerous sports – white-water rafting, mountaineering, skydiving – if properly done, injury is not inevitable, nor even likely. In a few of these sports, courting but escaping injury is part of the excitement. But in boxing, injury is the very point. The opponents aim to damage more than they are damaged; the best outcome each hopes for is to knock the other out.

Each blow to the head, even with padded gloves and head-guard, sends a shock wave through the gelatinous matter of the brain. Each blow can harm the brain tissues, either cata-strophically, as when a life-threatening blood clot forms, or in the way of small tears and bruises. These latter never heal, but worsen over time, for once brain scarring occurs it con-tinues to build, eventually leaving many boxers – studies show up to 40 per cent of them – with chronic progressive enceph-alopathy, the most usual form of which is *dementia pugilistica* (punch-drunkenness). Symptoms of damage can appear after a particularly hard bout, but on average only become fully manifest sixteen years from the end of a boxer's career. They include memory loss, slurred speech, tremors, a stumbling gait, stooping, facial rigidity, confusion, mood swings, rages, delusions and morbid jealousy. Boxers typically show abnormal MRI scans revealing enlargement of the fluid ventricles in the brain, and engrossment of the cerebral folds.

Still: like most avocations that cause brain damage, including drinking and its less legal alternatives, boxing is a highly pleasurable activity, and only involves willing participants. What the City men do with their spare time is therefore their own business. And some – for society is a polarised thing, where wealth and opportunity are unfairly distributed – doubtless think they deserve a smack on the head anyway.

The Meroe Augustus

Numismatists have a field day with the Roman crisis whose result was the triumph of Octavian, renamed Augustus. Personal portraits on coins became the norm with Julius Caesar, when he was amassing money for his Parthian campaign in 44 BC. The coins bore the legend 'Julius Caesar, Perpetual Dictator'. In the decades following his death Pompey, Octavian and Antony all issued their own portrait coins, counters in their deadly game of ambition. Coin portraits were contemporary and immediate; busts and statues tended to be memorial items, and anyway never reached as wide an audience.

Caesar's numismatic hubris was a factor in his failure. But by the time Augustus was emperor, the public-relations necessity of impressing himself on his far-flung and disparate subjects called for more than coin images or busts in the prevailing Greek memorial style. It needed contemporary images sending a strong message. On the way to apotheosis, Augustus had to convey a vivid sense of his energy, watchfulness and strength.

The Meroe head is a striking example of this new form of coercive portraiture. The alert head of a young man with emphatic, wide-open eyes staring at something slightly to one side, bespeaks a force not to be trifled with. Something in the head's expressive combination of youthfulness and austerity, something in the manic, even maniac, sharpness of the wide-eyed stare, thrills the viewer with the realisation that this strange man commands the world's most powerful army, and has no compunctions.

The Meroe Augustus is a symbol of the death of a project

which mattered greatly to the best minds of its age. This is best explained by remembering another great Roman, Cicero, who lived during the final years of the Republic, witnessing Caesar's dictatorship and Rome's collapse into a power struggle between rivals who wanted not to restore the vigorous Republican virtues but merely to fill Caesar's shoes. Cicero saw any form of autocracy as equivalent to slavery; so he quitted Rome when Caesar became dictator, retiring to his estate at Tusculum, where he then wrote the great works for which posterity, and especially the Renaissance, so admired him.

Cicero believed in the autonomy of the human individual, in the liberty to think and decide for oneself, in the existence of human rights, and in the responsibilities that rights entail. He viewed all men as brothers, and as capable of being guided by reason – a fact which, he argued, conferred on them a duty to develop themselves fully and to treat others with respect and generosity.

The world desired by Cicero was smashed in the Caesarian crisis, and Augustus's unflinching and uncompromising star – I think he might be looking with hostility at (say) a bust of Cicero, thinking: 'That tiresome old liberal windbag' – tells us that it would be a long time before anything approaching a Ciceronian world (parts of the contemporary West at least aspire to be such) returned.

The Crisis of Thought

Europe's long half-century between 1850 and the outbreak of the First World War is standardly divided into unequal portions, respectively characterised by increasing prosperity and Biedermeier complacency in the first twenty years, followed by the slow, rich, industrialised gearing-up towards total war in the remaining period, as newly unified portions of the continent jostled with older comities – not just along actual borders but in the far corners of the European-colonised globe. From London's Great Exhibition in 1851 to the birth of the German Empire in 1871 prosperity raised the European mood onto what Asa Briggs called 'the great plateau' between preceding and succeeding decades that were neither so easy nor so confident – decades of painful change beforehand, in which many suffered desperate hardship as industrialisation closed its grip everywhere, and succeeding decades of increasing instability as the old Vienna Congress diplomatic agreements broke down, franchises extended, and the *'bourgeois conquérant'* (to use Charles Moraze's phrase) grew increasingly uneasy at the prospect of socialism and science threatening, in one combined sweep, to upset their physical and spiritual economies. And as they feared, all collapsed at last into the cacophonies of Schoenberg, the incoherence of Cubism, the guns of August 1914, and the dire consequences of their thunder.

This picture is of course too simple, although not wholly inaccurate. Below the surface – a surface somewhat smoothed in its earlier part by the weight of organised capital's victory – there was tumultuous dissent and change. It is a striking

252 The Heart of Things

reflection that the fat years of the century's third quarter were launched by the revolutions of 1848–9. Both they and the increasingly pervasive liberal sentiment in western European politics were the remote consequences of a project begun another long half-century before, in 1789, at the gates of the Bastille. But that is how history works: the age of liberal democracy and market capitalism had its umbilicus cut by the defenders of the barricades in those 1848 uprisings, and the people who manned them – men such as Bakunin and Richard Wagner – were freed by defeat to dream other dreams with even greater consequences later.

Discussion of the long half-century before 1914 must begin with the revolutionary period prompted by the hard years before 1848. The inspiration for the 1848 uprisings was the desire to accomplish, without the terrors, the hopes of 1789, but their failure left a temporarily disillusioned intelligentsia seemingly powerless against the banausic strength of the new order. Historian J. M. Burrows has made the intriguing suggestion that in failing to achieve its ends by direct action, the spirit of that age sought to do so by a cleverly different means, equally utopian: the attempt to find unification and liberation – this time of intellectual kinds – through the progress and promise of natural science. The aim was to understand and control not merely material phenomena, but also the mind, for this was the time when sociology, psychology, and theories of social evolution were in their optimistic infancy. Combined with a strongly Whig view of history's upward trend, forms of perfectibilism were taken for granted and influenced thinking about human nature – not least, in making mankind the pinnacle of creation, at last able to understand the conditions of its own existence.

As is inevitable when reach exceeds grasp, this aspirational endeavour met with disillusionment too, and with strong negative reactions by many to the threats they perceived or imagined in science. Most of these many were also suspicious of the idea of scientific social progress, which they saw not as liberating but isolating, not as promoting human values but as denying and reducing them, because – in their view – it takes people out of the network of relationships that give human life meaning, and inflates the importance of the individual, who, on inspection, turns out to be hollow when removed from that network.

One result of this scepticism and anxiety was a quest for inner sources of value. For uneducated people these were found in religious revivalism and evangelicalism. In the case of intellectuals, a parallel turn to the inner took the form of commitment to theories about the Dionysian, as Nietzsche would have it, or the Unconscious, as Freud came to think of it – in either case, belief in the energising power of something non-rational, free and potentially creative, traits whose cultivation came to be seen as both the goal and the hallmark of the intellectual.

Histories of the movement of ideas in this period do better when they reflect not what later came to be seen as important, but what seemed important to contemporaries. A healthy corrective is introduced by this perspective, for we are inclined to think, *post facto*, that what Michelson and Morley were discovering about the luminiferous ether is far more important than what contemporaries thought of George Sand's novels, then huge best-sellers but now unread. Of course, it is impossible to ignore the racial theories of Gobineau or the views of Sorel and Marx on labour. But they cannot adequately be understood out of their context, which to contemporaries had a quite different contour.

This method has its risks and difficulties. Consider the impact on contemporaries of the Futurist Manifesto written by Filippo Marinetti: 'A racing car ... is more beautiful than the Winged Victory of Samothrace ... Beauty now exists only in struggle ... We want to glorify war – the world's only hygiene – militarism, patriotism, the destructive act of the anarchists, the beautiful ideas for which one dies, and contempt for women. We want to destroy museums, libraries and academies of all kinds ... We shall sing the great crowds excited by work, pleasure or rioting ...' These puerilities were published in 1909, and a history written from the contemporary point of view would give them a hearing they scarcely deserve by making them seem to be related, even in some formative way, to movements which included the Fauves, Cubists, atonal composers, early Kandinsky and Kokoschka, 'The Bridge' group of Dresden artists, and the like. No doubt it is an expression – a rather silly one – of a temper of the times which, in its larger scope, helps to explain the ebullient variety of these innovations, which bear a family resemblance to one another because of their joint historical conditioning; but it is hard to imagine that strainings after effect, and deliberate attempts to shock and be novel, were any less transparent then than they are now. The Manifesto caused a stir, but rather in the way that Damien Hirst's formaldehyde farm animals do – collapsing into historical quirks, as egregious examples of what people try on (according to Andy Warhol's definition: 'Art is what you can get away with'), in which there is rarely anything new or of value. It is of course hard to sort mere gesture from what produces a profound resonance in its own time, but one test is to ask: What would anyone of intelligence make of this, whether then or now? – for relativism is far from unrestrictedly true.

When one sees what was being said and written, and where it was tending in its increasing rush towards the smash of 1914, one sees that the staid accounts of nineteenth-century history we grew accustomed to in our formative years simply will not do, for they leave out the blood and sinews of a time which has much to answer for – the blood and sinews consisting of ideas, the true stuff of history, and the source of all its triumphs and tragedies.

Simplicity

It was once thought that the only way to explain the world's complexities, chief among them the amazing intricacy of life itself, is to say that the universe and everything in it was made by an intelligent designer. This heroic solution overlooked the fact that it solves one mystery by inventing a greater one, namely where the intelligent designer comes from. Was he (or she, or perhaps they) made by yet another intelligent designer? The problem is well illustrated by the story of the old lady who interrupted an astronomy lecture on the origins of the universe by saying, 'Young man! This Big Bang talk is rot. The universe sits on the back of a giant tortoise.' When the astronomer patiently asked what the tortoise in turn sits on, she replied, 'Aha! I've got you there! It's tortoises all the way down.'

From the time of Galileo and Newton onwards scientists sought to understand the world in terms of laws and regularities, expressed in a set of basic principles which capture the patterns of nature. The ideas thus developed were tested by seeing how successfully they predict future observations. But the assumption that order and simplicity rule nature sits in tension with the irregularities, asymmetries and diversities that nature so obviously contains. Do these latter somehow arise from the former? If so, how? The answer to the first question is Yes, and science is currently endeavouring to answer the second.

The secret is the nature of non-linear feedback processes. Scientific understanding of such processes is a recent achievement, made possible by the confluence of a number of different discoveries in the last century and more. At its heart lies the mathematical concept of chaos. Applying it to complex systems seemingly as diverse as the weather, earthquakes and the development of embryos shows something dizzying in its purport: that complex phenomena, including life, emerge from simple underlying phenomena in ways that result in self-organising systems maintaining themselves in states far from equilibrium (which literally means: balancing critically on the edge of chaos) by flows of energy from external sources – in the case of humans, the energy from the food they eat; in the case of life on earth overall, the energy from the sun. Thus the central concepts of chaos and complexity explain the emergence of phenomena that are far more than the sum of the simple parts which underlie them.

The computer has given a massive boost to the study of these questions. By simulating and modelling natural processes from evolution by natural selection to the behaviour of unstable piles of sand, scientists have found that chaotic behaviour, in the technical sense of behaviour which manifests critical sensitivity to very small changes either in initial conditions or as a result of feedback, is present everywhere in nature. The classic example is the weather, and indeed the fundamental idea of chaos is standardly illustrated by such examples as a butterfly in Brazil causing a tempest in Taiwan just by flapping its wings.

But what chaos theory shows is that chaos and order are mutually related and symbiotically dependent. Consider an example of a pile of sand to which further grains are added in a steady stream, as in an hourglass. The pile of sand grows erratically, and sand-slides constantly occur; but their effect is to maintain the sand pile in a state of delicate equilibrium, close to the verge of collapse. The scientist who first described this phenomenon, Per Bak, called it 'self-organising criticality'. Order is maintained by the concatenation of many small chaotic events each on a knife-edge of instability; think of the little slippages of sand as grains dislodge other grains, the symmetric-seeming pile a fragile whole with many mini-avalanches and a few big ones occurring constantly.

In fact the sand pile's avalanches are 'scale-free' in the sense that both small and large events are exactly the same in every particular except size. This is a standard feature of chaotically ordered systems as diverse as stock markets and earthquakes. Above all, it is a feature of life on earth, as described in James Lovelock's 'Gaia' theory. The world as a single ecosystem is always balanced on the edge of criticality, its overall stability (which survives extinctions and such catastrophes as collisions with asteroids) sustained by constant local chaos. Indeed, life would not be possible without the interplay between the rigidities of determinism at the simple level and the choices, possibilities and opportunities provided by chaos at the overall level.

If it is possible to be more filled with admiration for science and delight at the world it investigates, contemplation of the way chaos gives birth to order achieves both.

What Next?

Progress in social and economic matters is a relative notion. No country in the world is free of problems; rich Western democracies experience racial tensions, serious crime, underclass poverty, and polarised debates on moral questions. But Western poverty is not Third World poverty, and racial tensions in America are not the ethnic conflicts of Rwanda. So although progress is relative, it is real; and the world's more progressive polities show, through their history and institutions, what offers the best chance for forging a more stable, peaceful and prosperous world.

Talk of peace and prosperity smacks of pious cliché. In fact it is anything but. Which would you prefer: machine-gun fire in the next street, fear, danger – or warmth in winter, holidays in summer, a good job, hope, enjoyment? If the answer is obvious, why should the peace-and-prosperity alternative be yours alone? After all, if other people in other countries are shooting to kill, or starving to death, with neither the time nor resources to buy what you sell, what good does it do you? So even on the crassest self-interest, talk of peace and prosperity is not pious cliché but the statement of an urgent necessity.

Thus we return to the empirical question, 'What makes for peace and prosperity?' The answer is extremely well known. Democracy, human rights, the rule of law, and active promotion of fair opportunities for all – such are the minimum ingredients for a responsible and flourishing comity. There are few peaceful and prosperous places in the world where these minima are absent. In the domains of tyrants there might exist the peace of the prison-cell; and tyrants themselves, sitting atop their local food-chains, might sport diamond tie-pins; but such are mere simulacra of the real thing.

Societies can be truly peaceful and prosperous only on the basis of the institutional arrangements mentioned – democracy, rights, law, and opportunity. These are constitutive of what, for brevity, is called 'liberal democracy'. If the trends of the last two centuries, and especially of the last half-century, can be trusted, liberal democracy is spreading and succeeding, though it makes bow-waves of turbulence in its progress, as now, when it meets and disturbs social arrangements such as those central to traditional Islam. It does so because its central ideas of human equality, autonomy and participation are inconsistent with trad-itional, and especially theocratic, dispensations. The contrast between the positions of women in liberal democracies and traditional societies offers an especially sharp test; for it is no accident that poor and backward societies are almost invariably those in which women are uneducated, unempowered and pol-itically marginal.

A worst-case scenario for the imminent future is that the current backlash against the spread of liberal democracy defeats liberal democracy. This is not unimaginable, because although some of the liberal democracies have the world's biggest guns, all history (but especially recent history) shows that big guns are useless against guerrillas and terrorists, who between them can paralyse a liberal democracy, rob it of its liberality, and reduce its citizens to self-imprisoners – thereby achieving the same effect as the tyranny from which most of the enemies of liberal democracy come.

The best-case scenario is that the votaries of liberal democracy aim, and work, to share all its benefits with everyone, leaving no one out, and achieving their aim while protecting diversity in the best that all cultures have to offer – in art, music, cuisine, the celebrations of life and the nuances of pleasure. This is not a utopian goal; it is realisable, though it requires will. Looking at the aid budgets of the rich countries and the ever-widening gap between the rich and poor parts of the world shows that the will is completely lacking. Since in the end the will in question is that of individual tax-payers in rich countries, enlightened governments would do well to point out to their tax-payers that in their own crassest self-interest they need to buy a safer future for themselves.

The poor part of the world does not need hand-outs, but investment; not pity, but expertise; not patronage, but access to markets in the rich world. The systematic refusal of the rich world to let the poor world sell its products on equal terms in its markets is the single most serious block to development. That too is a matter of will. So the answer to the question, 'What next?' is: 'It depends on how willing we are to become wise, and to do right.'

Concluding Thoughts

The Uses of Philosophy

Modern times are a puzzle. Most people in Western countries are richer and healthier than they have ever been. Their lives are made easy by gadgets which cook their food, wash their clothes and warm their houses in winter. Their lives are made pleasant by other gadgets which entertain them, keep them in touch with their families, and transport them with swift convenience from home to work and back.

Yet according to many observers, people are less happy and fulfilled than their forebears. They feel discontented. There is a vacuum at the centre of their lives. A persistent frustration nags them, and they cannot identify its source. All they know is that the more gadgets and money they have, the more they feel the need for something to supply their lives with meaning or at least solace.

Some turn to the traditional resources of drugs (mainly in the form of alcohol or Prozac) or religion, both of which erect a safety barrier against discontent, although by different means – the first by obliterating consciousness of the vacuum, the latter by supplying a ready-made filling. Others hope to find the solution in love and family life, but find matters made worse by the failure of their expectations. Some turn to one of the many kinds of psychotherapy on offer, from Freudian psychoanalysis to behavioural therapy; or they seek relief in astrology, feng-shui, crystals, aromatherapy and tarot readings.

All these efforts have something in common. They are based on the belief that the problem of life's meaning can be solved by one or another nostrum from a new-age shop or a doctor's surgery, a counsellor or a pub, a church or a séance. By handing over either their money or their credulity at one of these places, they hope, they will be relieved of the emptiness within.

But another thing these efforts have in common is how often they fail. They might seem to work for a time, but like most mere coverings they become worn or frayed, and the shape of the original problem starts to show through. And it frequently happens that the original problem is harder to bear after an intermission of hope, because disappointment at the failure of the nostrum, and despair of finding a better alternative, add themselves to it.

Yet the best resource for dealing with the problem of the inexplicable void at the heart of rich, healthy, safe, well-fed, well-entertained modern Western life lies very close to hand, either unnoticed or, when noticed, neglected. In fact, modern Westerners are like thirsty people drinking from a muddy puddle on the banks of a great river of clear water, as if they simply had not noticed the river's existence, or did not know they could drink from it. The river in question is philosophy.

For two and a half thousand years Western civilisation has produced a succession of great thinkers who dedicated themselves to enquiring into what matters most in human existence. They sought, and offered, answers to such questions as: What is truly valuable? How should one live? What is the nature of the good? How should we understand love, death, grief, hope, freedom, truth, justice, beauty – and how should we live according to that understanding? What must we do to live courageously and successfully? How should we treat others? What are our duties as an individual, a citizen, a member of the human community? What are the rights we humans have? How might we best respect the world we live in? These questions overlap; the answers to them jointly define the life truly worth living.

Astonishingly, although most people at one time or another ask themselves some of these questions, they almost never turn to the immensely rich tradition of philosophical debate to see what our culture's greatest minds have said about them. There are many reasons for this, but chief among them are laziness and timidity. To seek out the writings of the philosophers, and to read them with attention, seems alarming because either it will be 'too difficult', or will involve too much hard work – the latter even more so when enquirers learn, as they early do, that central to the philosophical enterprise is the responsibility to think for oneself. All the great philosophers from Aristotle to Immanuel Kant have insisted on the fundamental importance of independent thought, because there is a world of difference between reaching a conclusion on your own, after considering the best that has been said on the matter, and simply accepting the say-so of someone else. The former sticks; it is your own; you worked for it. The latter (unless brainwashed into one early in life) is weakly attached, and soon falls away; it is second-hand. This is the difference between values and goals chosen by yourself on the basis of careful thought, and the nostrums sold in church or purchased at the new-age shop.

The key point here concerns the difference between autonomy, which in this connection means 'independence and self-motivation', and heteronymy, which means 'yielding responsibility to someone or something outside oneself'. Alcohol, Prozac, religion, feng-shui and the rest are all external solutions, easily taken off-the-shelf. People have become used to the idea that every problem can be dealt with in this way. Such solutions take the form of a 'technological fix': some practice or method will do the work for us. Thus we assume that science will solve environmental problems, that proper education will overcome social problems – and, in the case of personal difficulties, that a pill or a belief, a therapy or prayer, will do the trick. In all these cases we do not have to make any effort of our own. It is like dieting: we look for a fat-busting pill, or liposuction or stomach-stapling, something externally imposed, demanding from us no will power, no determination, no effort or labour. But unless we do the work needed for arriving at our choices, conclusions and aims, making them fully our own, and unless we use the best available materials for thinking about them, we will never truly attain any solutions worth having.

From its earliest flowering in Greek classical antiquity, philosophy has operated on the principle that the pursuit of truth and understanding must be free, open-minded, and autonomous. It therefore differs, in its very basis, from the usual way people come by their outlook, which is by submitting their intellects to the authority of pre-packaged, conventionally accepted beliefs. Philosophy examines the validity of every belief to see which is good and which is spurious. Only this way, say the philosophers, can humanity hope to attain enlightenment. And 'enlightenment', as the great eighteenth-century thinker Immanuel Kant wrote, 'is man's emergence from his self-imposed immaturity. Immaturity is the inability to use one's understanding without guidance from another. This immaturity is self-imposed when its cause lies not in lack of understanding, but in lack of resolve and courage to use it without guidance from another. *Sapere aude*! (Dare to know) – "Have courage to use your own understanding!" – that is the motto of enlightenment.'

In the rich and fascinating tradition of philosophy there are various schools of thought, and individual philosophers have often put forward views which conflict with those of other philosophers. The point is not that there are final answers in philosophy which one can accept, like buying a ready-made coat; to think this way is simply to repeat the mistake of hand-me-down nostrums. What the philosophers agree about is that we have to think things through for ourselves, taking the different sides of every problem into account; and they offer wide-ranging, in-depth perspectives on how to do so.

When people raise their heads from the muddy puddles of conventional 'solutions' to the problems of life, and see the river flowing nearby, they might of course still not drink from it, prevented by the factors already mentioned, namely timidity or laziness. Is the river too deep? Isn't swimming hard work? But if they accept the invitation of philosophy, they are usually delighted and surprised as a result. There are few worthwhile things that do not require us to make an effort to appreciate them, but the rewards always repay the effort. This is especially true of philosophy.

Here, by way of example, is what one of the most accessible of popular philosophers, Marcus Aurelius, has to say on the subject of something we all need at the core of our lives: tranquillity. 'Men seek retreats for themselves: houses in the country, at the seashore, in the mountains. Such is the desire of the most common sort of men. But it is in our power, whenever we choose, to retreat into ourselves. For nowhere either with more quiet or freedom do we retreat than into our own minds, particularly when we have within us such thoughts that by looking into them we are immediately perfectly tranquil. And this I affirm: tranquillity is nothing other than the proper ordering of the mind.'

Russell's History of Western Philosophy

Almost all those who reviewed Russell's now-famous *History of Western Philosophy* when it first appeared in 1945 were agreed about two things: first, that it is beautifully written, witty, clear, lucid and magisterial; and second, that it is not always accurate in its account of the thinkers it covers, nor always fair to them.

Even a cursory look at any page of the book testifies to the soundness of the first judgement, which shows how well both the book and the judgement have weathered the test of time. It has to be admitted that the second stands up too, and therefore Russell's frequently swift and sometimes cavalier treatment of his predecessors has worn less well. But despite the book's encyclopaedic title, he did not set out to write a neutral account. As he puts it himself in the Introduction, 'My purpose is to exhibit philosophy as an integral part of social and political life, not as the isolated speculations of remarkable individuals.' Because he could not be a mere neutral in social and political matters, he could not see philosophy's past, even its remote past, as being separable from questions which bear on the health of human thought and life.

History of Western Philosophy began life as a series of lectures given at the Barnes Foundation in Pennsylvania in the years 1941–3. In this guise it had a deeply troubled beginning, for Russell's life and fortunes were at a nadir during this period. Because of the war he was in a self-imposed exile in the United

States, hoping to keep his three children safe by bringing them up there. He had accepted appointments at Chicago University and then at the University of California at Los Angeles, but was unhappy at both places. He was pleased therefore to be offered an appointment at the City College in New York, to begin in the spring of 1940, and was just about to it take it up when successful legal efforts to have the appointment rescinded were made by a coalition of New York's Catholic and conservative finest. The coalition objected to his views about morals, especially as set out in his book *Marriage and Morals*, where he takes a notably liberal line in connection with sex, marital infidelity and homosexuality. (This book was singled out in his Nobel Prize citation in 1950, showing how time brings in its revenges.)

Although liberal opinion was fiercely behind Russell in his battle with the New York reactionaries, withdrawal of the post meant that he was in a parlous state, jobless and far from home with a wife and three children to support. In the circumstances even his supporters were disinclined to help, among them Harvard University, which pusillanimously refused to risk the wrath of Boston Catholics by giving him a post.

At this juncture the eccentric multi-millionaire art collector and ex-industrialist Dr Albert C. Barnes came unexpectedly to the rescue, offering Russell an appointment at his Foundation in Merion, Pennsylvania. The Barnes Foundation was an art and education institute run on idiosyncratic lines by Barnes himself, who prescribed all its rules down to the last detail. The idea of employing Russell was not Barnes's own, although when it was suggested to him by the philosopher John Dewey he delightedly agreed. Dewey had taught at the Barnes Foundation, and had remained on good enough terms with Barnes – quite a feat – to suggest this expedient for Russell's rescue. Knowing Barnes as he did, Dewey also advised Russell to ensure that he made every detail of his contract with Barnes completely precise at the outset. It proved excellent advice.

Trouble began in the first instance not between Russell and

Barnes but between the latter and Russell's wife Peter, by all accounts a difficult and supercilious woman who offended people – especially Americans – by insisting, as Russell himself never did, on the use of her aristocratic title. But in the increasingly difficult atmosphere Barnes and Russell themselves eventually fell out, and Barnes sought to dismiss Russell on the grounds that his lectures were below standard. The result was a court case, in which Russell gave the judge the manuscript of his *History of Western Philosophy* to read as proof of the quality of his work. The judge found in his favour.

By this time Russell had signed, on handsome terms, a contract for the book with the publishing house Simon and Schuster, and because the scandal surrounding his name from the New York affair had died down, he was again able to engage in lucrative journalism and lecturing. The book was accordingly finished in far better circumstances than it had begun, and was duly published just as the war ended.

The book begins with the Presocratic philosophers and follows the story of philosophy in the Western world right to the twentieth century, with Russell alluding to his own views at the end. No important figure is neglected, and many are included who would not normally figure in histories of philosophy. Throughout, but especially in the early parts, Russell places the philosophical developments he discusses in their historical settings. This is one of the most valuable aspects of the book. The earliest philosophers are described against the background of the rise of Greek civilisation, and the thought of the medieval Schoolmen is prefaced by an account of the papacy in the Middle Ages, and of the impact of the rise and spread of Islam. Indeed, every major division of the book is prefaced by an account of the historical background necessary to understanding the currents of thought it describes, and not a few readers of *History of Western Philosophy* will have acquired their first sense of the general sweep of Western history from Russell's panorama of it.

Russell had both a love of history, in which he read widely, and a genuine talent for writing historical narrative. Although not a coal-face historian in the sense of one who examines original documents in the search for data, his beautifully clear and lucid prose was a marvellously effective instrument for painting the broad sweep of events, and his sharp eye picked out exactly the right ones to relate. Russell's gifts as a writer were thus put as effectively to work in this respect as in his strictly philosophical endeavours. It is now less well known than it should be that one of his best books is indeed an historical work, *Freedom and Organisation*, describing the century between the battle of Waterloo and the outbreak of the First World War.

With his encyclopaedic grasp of the historical background to Western philosophy, Russell was able to choose the right framework for explaining the development of ideas and theories within it. For example, the section of the book dealing with modern philosophy from Machiavelli to Hume contains masterly vignettes on the Renaissance, the Reformation, and the rise of science – and as so often, he hit upon interesting adjuncts to the tale while doing so, in the case of science emphasising the vital importance to its progress of an entirely practical matter: the devising of new and better instruments for observing both the large and the small things in nature. The breadth of his grasp enabled him to offer significant insights. In his chapter on Machiavelli he says:

It is interesting to observe how the political thought of the Greeks and Romans, in their republican days, acquired an actuality in the fifteenth century which it had not had in Greece since Alexander or in Rome since Augustus. The Neoplatonists, the Arabs, and the Schoolmen took a passionate interest in the metaphysics of Plato and Aristotle, but none at all in their political writings, because the political systems of the age of City States had completely disappeared. The growth of City States in Italy synchronised with the revival of learning, and made it possible for humanists to profit by the political theories of republican Greeks and Romans.

It is also of more than merely passing interest that at several places in the book Russell alludes to the historical context in which it was being written – which means, to the Second World War actually raging about him. Talking of what things might be like, or should be like, after the war, Russell says that the Eastern world (China, Japan and India particularly) should be admitted on equal footing with the Western world, even though this will change the nature of civilisation in both parts of the world in unforeseeable but inevitable ways.

Throughout the book Russell's genius for the succinct, biting, often witty encapsulation of others' views is exploited to the full, to the delight of readers; but to critics the result sometimes seems too glib, slick and shallow to be informative. An excellent example both of his style and his manner is afforded by his discussion of the early twentieth-century French thinker Henri Bergson, whose views he here compares with those of Heraclitus and the Eleatics in antiquity:

> Zeno belonged to the Eleatic school, whose object was to prove that there could be no such thing as change. The natural view to take of the world is that there are things which change; for example, there is an arrow which is now here, now there. By bisection of this view, philosophers have developed two paradoxes. The Eleatics said that there were things but no changes; Heraclitus and Bergson said there were changes but no things. The Eleatics said there was an arrow, but no flight; Heraclitus and Bergson said there was a flight but no arrow. Each party conducted its argument by refutation of the other party. How ridiculous to say there is no arrow! say the 'static' party. How ridicu-

lous to say there is no flight! say the 'dynamic' party. The unfortunate man who stands in the middle and maintains that there is both the arrow and its flight is assumed by the disputants to deny both; he is therefore pierced, like Saint Sebastian, by the arrow from one side and by its flight from the other. But we have still not discovered wherein lies the force of Zeno's argument.

This account has all of Russell's distinctive strengths: the incisive brevity, the wry humour, the elegance, and what critics call the 'quickness', by which they mean insufficient detail and discussion. For the purposes Russell had in mind, the first three characteristics matter most, and they are certainly the chief reasons why *History of Western Philosophy* is so stimulating and entertaining. But readers should also be prepared to regard his reports of philosophers' views as being his own distinctive 'take' on them, with it frequently being the case that other commentators on those same philosophers might disagree with his interpretations of what they said or meant, and with the importance therefore of reading the original texts – if one is serious about philosophy – needing re-emphasis. With engaging frankness Russell never claimed to be a scholar of the works of any of the philosophers he describes, save for Gottfried Leibniz, about whom he wrote his first full-length philosophical work, and whose approach to philosophy had a large influence on Russell's own thought. (This did not make him fond of Leibniz, though: 'Leibniz was somewhat mean about money,' he writes. 'When any young lady at the court of Hanover married, he used to give her what he called a "wedding present", consisting of useful maxims, ending up with the advice not to give up washing now that she had secured a husband. History does not record whether the brides were grateful.') But his pointed and incisive judgements about philosophical ideas, whether or not he was exactly right in attributing them to this or that individual, are always worth reading, so much so that the *History* amounts to a philosophical education in its own right, just as many philosophical beginners have found.

The closing three chapters of the book, respectively on William James, John Dewey, and the 'philosophy of logical atomism', together provide a brief illuminating glimpse into Russell's own philosophical outlook. He did not agree with James and Dewey about everything, but he was much influenced by them. He accepted James's view of the mind while rejecting his 'pragmatic' theory of truth and his views about religion. He accepted many of Dewey's views about social and educational matters, but again could not accept Dewey's version of the pragmatist theory of truth, and so takes the opportunity to set out his own alternative view. The last chapter of the book gives a brief statement of his 'logical atomist' position, which had been the inspiration for Ludwig Wittgenstein's early work too, in the form of the *Tractatus Logico-Philosophicus*. These chapters accordingly offer a valuable starting point for anyone planning to make a study of Russell's thought, which is complex both in the details of its earlier focus upon philosophical logic, and in the series of evolutions it went through when his attention turned more fully to the overlap between epistemology (the theory of knowledge) and the philosophy of science. This latter concern remained with Russell until his last major philosophical book, *Human Knowledge*, whose main ideas he was pondering even as he wrote the *History*.

Nothing could be more characteristic either of the man or his philosophy than the way Russell ends his gargantuan trawl through two and a half thousand years of philosophical thought. The remarks in question are every bit as significant now as they were when he wrote them in the midst of a great war:

In the welter of conflicting fanaticisms, one of the few unifying forces is scientific truthfulness, by which I mean the habit of basing our beliefs upon observations and inferences as impersonal, and as much divested of local and

temperamental bias, as is possible for human beings ...
The habit of careful veracity acquired in the practice of
this philosophical method can be extended to the whole
sphere of human activity, producing, wherever it exists,
a lessening of fanaticism with an increasing capacity of
sympathy and mutual understanding.

Since its publication, *History of Western Philosophy* has been
a best-seller, continuing to be read in quantity year after year,
and providing the starting point in philosophy for many. Because
of the partisan nature of its views and the quick, witty style of
their presentation, it has never been a staple as an academic
textbook. Instead it has belonged to the amateurs of philosophy,
in both the sense of those who love the pursuit and those who
read it in their own time and for their own instruction. Written
late in life by one of the great contributors to philosophy and
logic, who was also a man of deep and abiding liberal principles,
it is a unique book. Highly readable, very amusing, full of
instruction even when it needs the correctives of closer scholarship, it is one of the monuments of twentieth-century philosophy and literature, and deserves its place on the bookshelves
of anyone interested in Russell and philosophy.